ORGANIZING FOR WORK

Organizing for Work

By

Henry Laurence Gantt

ΑΩ
ENNA LEAN ORIGINS

Enna Products

1602 Carolina St.

Suite B3

Bellingham, WA 98229

Telephone: (360) 306-5369

Fax: (905) 481-0756

E-mail: info@enna.com

Library of Congress Cataloging-in-Publication Data

Gantt, Henry L., 1861-1919
  Organizing for Work
  Includes Index
  ISBN 978-1-897363-80-5

1. Lean manufacturing.   2. Organizational management.
3. Industrial efficiency.   I. Title.

ACKNOWLEDGMENTS

We would like to thank Jeff Maling of IBM and Norman Bodek of PCS Press for the motivation and inspiration to bring this classic work into the fold of Lean Manufacturing. We would also like to thank Tracy S. Epley for text layout and his efforts in editing an early 20th century book for 21st century readers, and Khemanand Shiwram for his creative flair in designing the cover and reproducing the original Gantt charts.

FOREWORD

This new edition of H. L. Gantt's classic, *Organizing for Work* was designed with the modern Lean manager in mind. For first time readers, you will gain new insights into why we strive to become Lean; for those familiar with the work, re-reading Chapter 2, "The Engineer as Industrial Leader" will renew your enthusiasm for your chosen craft. For both it will provide not only a deeper understanding of the origins and ethos of Lean Manufacturing, it will also give you a proven model for managing employees, production and improvement. One aspect of that model is our exclusive reproduction of the original charts used in this book. Easier to read and understand than the originals, and more thoroughly explained than current academic reprints, Enna's Gantt charts have clarified the purpose of their use. This is the only edition of an honored classic that takes the message out of the classroom and puts it the Lean context.

The growth of Lean as we know it today traces its roots back to 1929, when Kiichiro Toyoda witnessed production at a Ford assembly line and took information and ideas back to Japan. By 1938, Toyota had launched its Just In Time system on a full scale basis and for the next 50 years, the Toyota Production System (Lean) grew into a productive powerhouse that was hidden from the eyes of the world. Shigeo Shingo and Taiichi Ohno are considered the architects of modern Lean Manufacturing; their thoughts, sayings and methods are taught and applied everyday in industries around the globe. Where did their wisdom come from? Undoubtedly, much of it came from within Toyota as well as from each man's personal experiences, yet the cornerstones of Lean did not just appear out of thin air. With its emphasis on customer service, efficiency and bridging gaps between worker and management, *Organizing for Work* must have been in the curriculum of these gentlemen's education.

Henry Laurence Gantt was a mechanical engineer from Johns Hopkins University. An early associate of Frederick Taylor, Gantt parted ways with Taylor in terms of the human aspect of production. Where Taylor saw one best way for management to instruct staff, Gantt saw many ways for workers and management to work together for the mutual benefit of themselves and the business. Henry Gantt's familiarity with the war effort came from his association with Brigadier General William Crozier, Chief of Ordnance for the U.S. Army. Invited by General Crozier to streamline the production of munitions before the outbreak of war, Gantt's methods were so successful that the Ordnance Department was the most productive department in the armed forces. Further proof of Gantt's success was the adaptation of those same methods for use in the Emergency Fleet Corporation, although it was used to a lesser extent by those in authority because they were "better satisfied simply to report what they had done, rather than compare it too closely with what they might have done." This type of attitude has haunted American industry ever since.

Henry Gantt saw promise in the social movements of Europe, but the means to achieve those aims left him cold. As *Organizing for Work* makes clear, Gantt was a Christian and a patriot. He calls Christ, "the first great Economist" based on His understanding of "the commanding power of service." This means service to the community and service to humanity, not service to oneself. Through the revolutions and social unrest across Europe, Henry Gantt saw a way to achieve the same goals of the revolutionaries without the violence that revolutions invariably bring. In doing so we would preserve and strengthen the foundation of democratic service that made America a dynamic nation from the beginning. Henry Gantt's words, "our most serious trouble is incompetence in high places," carries forward his idea that democracy must not bow to autocratic methods. The manager who has not earned his position and is immune from responsibility will fail time and again, at the cost of the business and the workman, until there are no more excuses. At that point, those involved can only hope that there's a business left to salvage.

Gantt devised the charts that bears his name to know at a glance what stage production was in, as well as to gauge the efficiency of those doing the work. Modern usage of Gantt charts all but ignore this powerful feature of the chart; with only a few minutes of study the comprehensive nature of the Gantt chart gives a concise review of each workers performance. In turn, the same Gantt chart is used as a measure of foremen and management. This creates a strong, cohesive workforce which endeavors at all times to perform at their peak. A fundamental aspect of being human is the competitive spirit that compels all of us to be the best, or at the very least, to do our best. This competitive spirit is a gateway for improvement, as workers will not want "to advertise their incompetence to their fellows." Not only does this provide options for the worker, it also provides vital information to managers so they can utilize personnel for skill specific positions. It is this line of thinking, that workers are the masters of machines and not a part of them, that elevates Henry Gantt out of the history books and into modern Lean Manufacturing.

In this concise text lies the foundation of the second pillar of Lean Manufacturing — Respect For People. Henry Gantt realized the difficulties that confront management and workers, but difficulties are bread and butter for engineers. H. L. Gantt devised solutions that work. The Gantt chart, an important management tool for a century, is not Henry Gantt's most important contribution to industry. His legacy rests in his beliefs of customer service, fairness and in doing things right; this legacy was passed on to the modern fathers of the Lean Manufacturing movement, Taiichi Ohno and Shigeo Shingo.

I am proud to present you with one of the keystones of modern Lean Manufacturing. When this book is taken off the shelf and applied, it will invigorate any Lean Initiative. The American origins of Lean Manufacturing are indisputable; if we can take pride in our history and humility from the lessons we have learned, Lean Manufacturing will again become as American as baseball. As any good baseball manager knows, the fundamentals must be mastered in order to win. However, it is the great managers that know that fundamentals can never be mastered, they must become a continuous daily practice. Henry Gantt's *Organizing for Work* is a playbook no manager should be without.

Philip Goritsas
Vice President

PREFACE

The two greatest forces in any community are economic and political forces backed by military power. To develop the greatest amount of strength for the benefit of the community, they must work together, hence must be under one direction.

Germany had already accomplished this union before entering the war by having her political system practically take over the industrial; the Allies rapidly followed suit after the war began.

We soon discovered after entering the war that our political system alone was not adequate to the task before it. We supplemented it by a food administrator, a coal administrator, a war labor board, a war industries board, a shipping board, and others, which were intended to be industrial, and as far as possible, removed from political influences. There is no question that they handled their problems much more effectively than was possible under strictly political control.

The Soviet system is an attempt to make the business and industrial system serve the community as a whole, and in doing so, take over the functions of and entirely supplant the political system. Whether it can be made to work or not remains to be seen. Up to date it has failed, possibly because control has fallen into the hands of people of such extreme radical tendencies that they would wreck any system.

The attempt which extreme radicals all over the world are making to get control of both the political and business systems, on the theory that they would make the industrial and business system serve the community, is a real danger so long as our present system does not accomplish that end. This danger is real irrespective of the fact that they have as yet nowhere proved their case.

Is it possible to make our present system accomplish this end? If so, there is no excuse for such a change as they advocate, for the great industrial and business system on which our modern civilization depends is essentially sound at the bottom, having grown strong because of the service it rendered. Not until the business and industrial systems realized the enormous power it had gained through making itself indispensable to the community did it go astray by making the communities serve it. Business and industry then ceased to render service democratically and demanded autocratically that its will be done. "It made tools and weapons of cities, states, and empires." Then came the great catastrophe.

In order to resume our advance toward the development of an unconquerable democratic civilization, we must purge our economic system of all autocratic practices of whatever kind. To do this, we must return to the democratic principle of rendering service, which was the basis of its wonderful growth.

Unless within a short time we can accomplish this result, there is apparently nothing to prevent our following Europe into the convulsions of economic confusion which seem to threaten the very existence of its civilization.

Table of Contents

The Parting of the Ways

The existence of modern civilization is entirely dependent on the proper functioning of the industrial and
business systems. If these systems fail to function properly in any important particular, such as transportation or
coal mining, the large cities will in a short time be scarce of
food, and industry throughout the country will be brought to
a standstill for lack of power.

It is clear that the maintenance of modern civilization is absolutely dependant upon the service it gets from the industrial and business system.

This system, as developed throughout the world, had its origin in the service it rendered to the community in which it started. With the rise of better technology it was found that larger industrial aggregations could render more effective service than the original smaller ones. Naturally, the smaller ones gradually disappeared, leaving the field to those that could provide better service.

Such was the normal and natural growth of business and industry which obtained its profits because of its superior service. Toward the latter part of the nineteenth century it was discovered that a relatively small number of factories had replaced the numerous mechanics with their little shops, such as the village shoemaker and the village wheelwright. The community at large became dependent upon the relatively smaller number of larger establishments in each industry.

Under these conditions it was only natural that a new class of business man should arise. One who realized that if all the plants in any industry were combined under one control, the community would have to accept such service as it was willing to offer, and pay the price which it demanded. In other words, it was clearly realized that if such combinations could be made to cover a large enough field, they would no longer need to serve the community but could force the community to do their bidding. The Sherman Anti-Trust Law was the first attempt to curb this tendency. However, it was successful only to a very limited extent, for the idea that the profits of a business were justified only on account of the service it rendered was rapidly giving way to one in which profits took the first place and service the second. This idea has grown so rapidly and has become so firmly imbedded in the mind of the business man of today, that it is inconceivable to many leaders of big business that it is possible to operate a business system on the lines along which our present system grew up;

namely, that its first aim should be to render service.

This conflict of ideals is the source of the confusion into which the world now seems to be driving headlong. *The community needs service first, regardless of who gets the profits, because its life depends upon the service it gets.* The business man says profits are more important to him than the service he renders; that the wheels of business shall not turn, whether the community needs the service or not, unless he can have his measure of profit. *He has forgotten that his business system had its foundation in service, and as far as the community is concerned has no reason for existence except the service it can render.* A clash between these two ideals will ultimately bring a deadlock between the business system and the community. The "laissez faire"* process in which we all seem to have so much faith, does not promise any other result, for there is no doubt that industrial and social unrest is distinctly on the increase throughout the country.

Therefore, I say that we have come to the *Parting of the Ways*, for we must not drift on indefinitely toward an economic catastrophe such as Europe exhibits to us. We probably have abundant time to revise our methods and stave off such a catastrophe if those in control of industry will recognize the seriousness of the situation. Once recognized, they should promptly present a positive program which recognizes the responsibility of the industrial and business system to render such service as the community needs. The extreme radicals have always had a clear vision of the desirability of accomplishing this end, but they have always fallen short in the production of a mechanism that would enable them to materialize their vision.

American workmen will prefer to follow a definite mechanism which they can comprehend, rather than take the chance

---

*Laissez-faire, French for "let it be", is an economic theory in which the business of nations is best served with minimal government intervention.

of accomplishing the same end by the methods advocated by extremists. In Russia and throughout eastern Europe the community, through the Soviet form of government, is attempting to take over the business system in its effort to secure the service it needs. Their methods seem crude to us and violate our ideas of justice; but in Russia they replaced a business system which was rotten beyond anything we can imagine; it would not require a very perfect system to be better than what they had. The dealings of our manufacturers with Russian business agents during the war indicated that graft was almost the controlling factor in all deals. The Soviet government is neither Bolshevistic nor Socialistic, nor is it political in the ordinary sense; it is the first attempt to found a government on industrialism. Whether it will be ultimately successful or not remains to be seen. While the movement is going through its initial stages it is unquestionably working through great hardships, which are enormously aggravated by the fact that it has fallen under the control of extreme radicals. Would it not be better for our business men to return to the ideals upon which their system was founded upon and which it grew to such strength? Shouldn't rewards be dependent solely upon the service rendered, rather than to risk any such attempt on the part of the workmen in this country, even if we could keep it clear of extreme radicals, which is not likely? *We all realize that any reward or profit that business arbitrarily takes, over and above that to which it is justly entitled for service rendered, is just as much the exercise of autocratic power and a menace to the industrial peace of the world, as the autocratic military power of the Kaiser was a menace to international peace. This applies to Bolshevists as well as to Bankers.*

I am not suggesting anything new when I say reward must be based on service rendered. I am simply proposing that we go back to the first principles, which still exist in many rural communities where the newer idea of big business has not yet penetrated. Unquestionably many leading business men recognize this general principle and successfully operate their business accordingly. Many others would like to go back to it, if they saw how such a move could be accomplished.

Under the stress of war, it was clearly seen that a business and industrial system run primarily for profits could not produce the war gear needed. We promptly adopted a method of finance which was new to us; the Federal Government took over the financing of such corporations as were needed to furnish the munitions of war. The financial power of the Federal Government did not expect any profit from these organizations, but attempted to run them in such a manner as to deliver the greatest possible amount of goods.

The best known of these is the Emergency Fleet Corporation*. It is not surprising that such a large corporation developed in such great haste should have been inefficient in its operating methods, but there are reasons to believe that in the long run it will prove to have handled its business better than similar undertakings that were handled directly through the Washington bureaus. It gave us a concrete example of how to build a Public Service corporation, the fundamental fact concerning which is that it must be *financed by public money.* That it has not been more successful is due, not to the methods of its financing, but to the method of its operation. The sole object of the Fleet Corporation was to produce ships, but there has never been among the higher officers of the Corporation a single person, who, during the past twenty years, has made a record in production. They have all without exception been men of the "business" type of mind who have made their success through financing, buying, selling, etc. If the higher officers of the Fleet Corporation had been men who understood modern production methods, and had in the past been successful in getting results through their use, it is probable that the Corporation would have been highly successful, and would have given us a good example of how to build an effective Public Service corporation.

---

*Established by President Wilson in July 1917, the Emergency Fleet Corporation was created to establish a "bridge to France" across the German U-boat infested waters of the Atlantic. The first ship was completed in December of 1917, yet by Armistice Day of November 11, 1918, not one ship had yet to cross the Atlantic.

During the summer of 1917, the Chairman of the Federal Trade Commission, Mr. William B. Colver, explained how we might have a Public Service corporation for the distribution of coal. In such a corporation as Mr. Colver outlined there would be good pay for all who rendered good service, but no "profit." Of course, all those who are now making profits over and above the proper reward for service rendered in the distribution of coal opposed Mr. Colver's plan. His plan was that a corporation, financed by the Federal Government, should buy at the mouth of each mine such coal as it needed at a fair price based on the cost of operating that mine; this corporation would distribute to the community the coal at an average price, including the cost of distribution. We see no reason why such a corporation should not have solved the coal problem, and furnished us with an example of how to solve other similar problems. We need such information badly, for we are rapidly coming to a point where we realize that *disagreements between employer and employee as to how the profits shall be shared can no longer be allowed to work hardship to the community.*

The chaotic condition into which Europe is rapidly drifting by the failure of the present industrial and financial system emphasizes the fact that in a civilization like ours, the problems of peace may be quite as serious as the problems of war. The emergencies and needs created by these problems justify the same kind of action on the part of the government as was justified by war.

Before proper action can be taken in this matter it must be clearly recognized that the economic conditions of today have far more power for good or for evil than political theories. This has become so evident in Europe that it is impossible to fail much longer to recognize it here. The revolutions which have occurred in Europe, and the agitation which seems about to create other revolutions, are far more economic than political in nature, and hence can only be offset by economic methods.

The Labor Unions of Great Britain and the Soviet System of Russia both aim to render service to the community by different very methods. Whether they will be effective or not is uncertain, for they are revolutionary and a revolution is a dangerous experiment, the result of which can never be foreseen. The desired result can be obtained *without a revolution* and by methods with which we are already familiar, if we will only establish real public service corporations to handle problems which are of most importance to the community, and realize that capital, like labor, is entitled only to the reward it earns.

Inasmuch as the profits in any corporation go to those who finance that corporation, the only guarantee that a corporation is a true public service corporation is that it is financed by public money. If it is so financed then all the profits go to the community, and if service is more important than profits, it is always possible to get maximum service by eliminating profits altogether.

This is the basis of the Emergency Fleet Corporation as well as numerous other war corporations which rendered public service because it was impossible to get such service from private corporations. Realizing that on the return of peace many private corporations feel that they no longer have any such social responsibilities as they cheerfully accepted during the war, it would seem that real public service corporations would be of the greatest possible advantage in the industrial and business reorganization that is before us.

In this country we have a little time to think, because economic conditions here are not as acute as they are in Europe, and because of the greater prosperity of our country. But we must recognize the fact that our great, complicated system of modern civilization, whose existence depends upon the proper functioning of the business and industrial system, cannot be supported much longer unless the business and industrial system devotes its energies to rendering the service necessary to support it. We have no hesitation in saying that workmen cannot continue to get high wages unless they do a big day's work. *Is it not an equally self-evident fact that the business man cannot continue to get big rewards unless he renders a corresponding amount of service?* Apparently the similarity of these two propositions has not dawned upon the man with the financial type of mind, perhaps because he has never compared them. Such a change would produce hardships only for those who are getting the rewards they are not earning. It would be of great benefit those who are actually doing the work.

In order that we may get a clear idea of what such a condition would mean, let us imagine two nations as nearly identical as we can picture them. One nation had a business system based on and supported by the service it rendered to the community. Let us imagine that the other nation, having the same degree of civilization, had a business system run primarily to give profits to those who controlled that system, which rendered service when such service increased its profits, but failed to render service when such service did not make for profits. To make the comparison more exact, let us further imagine a large portion of the most capable men of the latter community engaged continually in a pull and haul, one against the other, to secure the largest possible profits. Then let us ask ourselves in what relative state of economic development these two nations would find themselves at the end of ten years? It is not necessary to answer this question.

I say again, then, we have come to the *Parting of the Ways.* A nation whose business system is based on service will in short order show such gains over one whose system is operated for the sole object of securing the greatest possible profits for the investing class, that the latter nation will not be long in the running.

America holds a unique place in the world, and by its traditions is the logical nation to continue to develop its business system on the line of service. What is happening in Europe should hasten our decision to take this step, for the business system of our country is identical with the business system of Europe, which, if we are to believe the reports, is so endangered by the crude efforts of the Soviets to make business serve the community.

The lesson is this: *the business system must accept its social responsibility and devote itself primarily to service, or the community will ultimately make the attempt to take it over in order to operate it in its own interest.*

The spectacle of the attempt to accomplish this result in Eastern Europe is certainly not so attractive as to make us desire to try the same experiment here. Hence, we should act, and act quickly, on the former proposition.

THE ENGINEER AS INDUSTRIAL LEADER

The principles explained in the preceding chapter may seem clear and simple enough to appeal to almost any enlightened person and give them the desire to carry them out. However, the desire to put them in operation is not enough. He must have at least some inkling of the methods by which their application can be made. He must understand the forces which he will have to contend with in introducing the newer methods; the arguments that will be brought up against them, and the obstacles that will be put in his way by those who are perfectly well satisfied to go on as they are, in spite of the fact that a change is seen to be absolutely necessary in the long run.

In the following chapters we shall try to give a picture of how business and industry are conducted, and some explanation of the forces controlling each. Most of our business and industrial troubles arise from the fact that the controlling factors are not readily apparent to the general public and can be fully disclosed only by an exhaustive study of what is taking place.

Following this general exposition of the subject, we will show a system of progress charts which bear the same relation to statistical reports that movies bear to a photographs. This chart system has been in use for a few years, but is so simple that it is readily understood by the workman and employer. The charts are so comprehensive that one intelligent workman made the remark, "If we chart everything we do that way, anybody could run the shop." While we are hardly prepared to agree with this opinion, we are entirely satisfied that if the facts about a business can be presented in a compact and comprehensive manner, it will be found possible to run any business much more effectively than has been the custom in the past.

We wish to emphasize the practicality of our methods because we have been accused of preaching altruism in business, which our critics say will not work. We know altruism will not work and absolutely repudiate the idea that our methods are altruistic; as a matter of fact, we believe we should get full reward for service rendered. More to the point, we believe that if everybody got full reward for service rendered there would not be so many "profits" for the employer and employee to quarrel over, so often to the detriment of the public.

With this introduction we shall try to make clear what has been happening in the industrial and business world and draw our conclusions as we go along.

When the war broke out, many of our leading business men who had accumulated wealth through accepted business methods of buying, selling, financing, etc., went to Washington and offered their services for a dollar a year. They did this with the best intentions, believing that the business methods which had brought them success in the past were the ones needed in time of war. They soon found that the government had taken over all financial operations; there was no selling to be done. The problem quickly reduced itself to one of production, in which many of them had no previous experience. Of course, there were many marked exceptions, for some grasped the problem at once and did wonderful work. As a general rule, however, this was not the case, for it takes a very capable man to quickly grasp the essence of a big problem that is new to him. Hence, as a rule, they adhered strictly to the methods that had brought them success and brought great numbers of accountants and statisticians (all static) to assist them. Both groups were thoroughly convinced that record-keeping was the main aim of business.

While the army was calling for ships, shells, trucks, and tanks, these men busied themselves with figures and statistics, apparently quite satisfied that they were doing their part. In many cases these statisticians did not differentiate between that which is interesting and that which is important. In only a few cases did they realize that, from the standpoint of production, yesterday's record is valuable only as a guide for tomorrow. They did not understand that it is only the man who knows what to do and how to do it that can direct the accumulation of the facts he needs for his guidance. In too many cases such men had been left behind to run the factories, while their superiors, who had no experience in production, undertook for the government the most important job of production we have ever had. They depended almost entirely upon accountants and statisticians for guidance. The results of their labors are now history, a knowledge of which will soon be the common property of all. In spite of this handicap, we still managed to do much good work.

There is no question that both our army and navy have made good to a degree which none of our allies anticipated. However, it is also true that if we had not had economic assistance from our allies, the results they have obtained would have been impossible. As a matter of fact, it is well known that our industrial system has not measured up to our own expectations. To substantiate this we have only to mention airplanes, ships, field guns, and shells. The reason our industrial system is falling short is undoubtedly because the men directing it had been trained in a business system operated only for profits, and did not comprehend one operated solely for production. This is no criticism of the men as individuals; they simply did not know the job, and, what is worse, they did not know they did not know it.

Inasmuch as our economic strength in the future will be based on production, we must modify our system as rapidly as possible, with the end result of putting producers in charge. To do this, opinions must give place to facts, and words to deeds. The engineer, who is a man of few opinions and many facts, few words and many deeds, should be accorded the leadership which is his proper place in our economic system.

It must be remembered that the engineer has two distinct functions. One is to design and build his machinery; the second is to operate it. In the past he has given more attention to the former function than to the latter. At first this was a natural and necessary condition because the various engineering structures were comparatively few and were operated in a simple and independent measure. However, now with the multiplicity of machines of all kinds, the operation of one is many times intimately dependent upon the operation of another, even in one factory. In addition to this, the operation of one factory is always dependent upon the successful operation of a number of others. Because this inter-operation is necessary to render service or produce results, the complexity of operating problems has greatly increased. The operation of a large number of factories in harmony presents much the same

14

problem as the harmonious operation of the machines in one factory. However, it is only where the factories have been combined under one management that any direct attempt at this kind of control has been made. To be sure, the relation between the supply and demand of the product, supplemented by a desire to get the greatest possible profit, has resulted in a sort of control. This control has usually been based more on opinion than facts, and exercised to secure the greatest possible profits rather than to render the greatest service.

Allow me to emphasize again the self-evident fact that great reward can only be sustained by corresponding service; and maximum service can be rendered only when actions are based on knowledge. We realize that the logical director for such work is the engineer. The engineer not only has a basic knowledge of the work, but his training and experience lead him to rely only upon facts. However, there is not in general use any mechanism that enables the engineer to visualize at once the large number of facts that must be comprehended in order to effectively handle the multitude of managerial problems that our modern industrial system is constantly facing. It is one object of this book to lay before the public the progress we have made in visualizing the problems and the available information needed for their solution.

Efficiency & Idleness

W hat we accomplished in our preparation for war and in getting our men to the front lines not only surprised ourselves but satisfied our allies as well. It was accomplished only by the splendid energy and tremendous resources of the American people, but nobody pretends that we were very efficient in doing the work. Our expenses were enormous and we reconciled ourselves to their magnitude by saying over and over again that nothing mattered except winning the war, which in the last analysis is true; but it is also true that excessive expenses hindered us in accomplishing this result.

Our fumbling in war preparation seems to indicate that the great campaign for efficiency, which has been waged so assiduously in this country for the past twenty years, has not accomplished for us all we had led ourselves to believe. That we have increased individual and profit-making efficiency, and perhaps other kinds of efficiency, is not to be denied. That we have attained a high degree of national efficiency or a high degree of efficiency in the production of goods, is nowhere indicated. It took the shock of a great war to arouse us to the realization that our great prosperity was due to something other than our productive efficiency.

Yet surely the long campaign for efficiency has been honestly and seriously waged. If this is true, then why have our results been so meager? The answer is simple enough and plain. The aim of our efficiency has not been to produce goods, but to harvest dollars. If we could harvest more dollars by producing fewer goods, we produced fewer goods. If it happened that we could harvest more dollars by producing more goods, we made an attempt to produce more goods: but the production of goods was always secondary to the securing of dollars.

In the great emergency created by the war, our need was not for dollars but for goods. The people who had been trained for the seeking of dollars were in most cases not at all fitted for the producing of goods. However, those who had been most successful in acquiring dollars were the ones best known as business men, and when it was thought we needed a business administration, such people, with the best intentions in the world, offered their services to the Federal Government, many at a great sacrifice of their own interests. However, they found that for war we needed goods, and that dollars were only the means to that end. Then they found that unless people knew how to produce the goods, dollars were ineffective.

Another phase of the efficiency movement with which we are all so familiar, was the attempt to increase the efficiency of the worker and to simply ignore the idler, because the system of cost-keeping generally in vogue made that seem the most profitable thing to do. The case was worse than this, for not only did the system ignore the idler, but it eliminated the inefficient, ignoring the fact that both the inefficient and the idle were going to continue to live and be supported, directly or indirectly, by the workers.

The war awoke us to the fact that the world was running short of the necessities of life, and that the product of even the most inefficient was of some help. The scheme for the selection of the efficient, of which much had been made, was now found to need supplementing by one for forcing the idler to work and training the inefficient.

The great difficulty of installing such a system was that the cost-keeping methods in vogue at the time indicated that training methods were not profitable, because trainers were classed as non-producers. On the other hand, in spite of this fact the war emergency forced us to adopt them, and the results were beneficial. The inevitable deduction is that the cost-keeping methods in general vogue are fundamentally wrong, and that we shall continue to suffer from inefficiency until they are corrected. The great error in them is the fact that they absolutely ignore the expense of idleness. As a matter of fact, it costs almost as much to be idle as it does to work. This is true whether we consider *men* or *machines*, or, in other words, *labor* or *capital*.

This leads us at once to two natural questions:

What is our expense for idle labor?

What is our expense for idle capital?

Manufacturing concerns generally eliminate idle labor as

completely as they can (many times by discharging work-men who could be profitably used if work were planned for them).

They cannot get rid of idle capital so easily, for it is tied up in machines that cannot be sold. The only possible way to eliminate idle capital is to put it to work. The first step to-ward putting it to work is to find out why it is idle. As soon as this is done, means for putting it to work begin to suggest themselves. In order to meet the present and any future emer-gencies, our cost keeping system must not content itself with charging all expenses to the product. Product price should re-flect only that expense which helped produce it. Furthermore, our cost-keeping system must show the causes of expenses that did not produce. If this fundamental change is made in our cost-keeping methods, our viewpoint on the subject of production changes, with the result that we devote our at-tention first to the elimination of idleness, both of capital and labor.

Production & Cost

Manufacturers recognize the vital importance in knowing the cost of their product, yet only a few of them have a cost system on which they are willing to rely on under all conditions.

While it is possible to get very accurate information on the amount of material and labor used directly in the production of an article, there does not yet seem to be any system of distributing that portion of the expense known as indirect expense, burden, or overhead. There are several methods in common use of distributing these expenses, but none that can provide any real confidence that it has been done properly. One is to distribute to the product the total sum of indirect expenses, including interest, taxes, insurance, etc., according to the direct labor. Another is to distribute a portion of this expense according to direct labor, and a portion to machine hours. Other methods distribute a certain amount of this expense on the material used, etc. Most of these methods contemplate the distribution of all of the indirect expense of the manufacturing plant on the output produced, no matter how small it is.

If the factory is running at its full, or normal, capacity, this item of indirect expense per unit of product is usually small. If the factory is running at only a fraction of its capacity, say one-half, and turning out only one-half of its normal product, there is little change in the total amount of this indirect expense. All of these expenses must now be distributed over half as much product as previously, each unit of product thereby being obliged to bear approximately twice as much expense as previously.

When times are good and there is plenty of business this method of accounting indicates that our costs are low; when times are bad and business is slack, it indicates high costs due to the increased proportion of burden each unit has to bear. During good times when there is demand for all the product we can make, it is usually sold at a high price and the element of cost is not such an important factor. When business is dull, however, we cannot get such a high price for our product. The question of how low a price can we afford to sell the product then becomes of vital importance. Our cost systems, as operated at present, show that under such conditions our costs are high and, if business is very bad, they usually show us a cost far greater than the amount we can actually get for the goods. In other words, our present systems of cost accounting go to pieces when they are needed most. This being the case, many have felt for a long time that there was something radically wrong with the present theories on the subject.

As an illustration, I cite a case which recently came to my attention. A man found that his cost on a certain article was thirty cents. When he found that he could buy it for twenty-six cents, he gave the orders to stop manufacturing and to start buying. He said he did not understand how his competitor could sell at that price. He realized that there was a flaw somewhere, but he could not locate it. I asked him what his expense consisted of and his reply was, labor ten cents, material eight cents, and overhead twelve cents. I then asked if he was running his factory at full capacity, and got the reply that he was running it at less than half its capacity, possibly at one-third. The next question was: What would be the overhead on this article if the factory were running full? The reply was that it would be about five cents. I suggested that in such a case the cost would be only twenty-three cents. The possibility that his competitor was running his factory full suggested itself at once as an explanation.

The next question that suggested itself was how the twelve cents overhead, which was charged to this article, would be paid if the article was bought. The obvious answer was that it would have to be distributed over the product still being made, and would thereby increase its cost. In such a case it would probably be found that some other article was costing more than it could be bought for; and, if the same policy were pursued, the second article should be bought, which would cause the remaining product to bear a still higher expense rate. If this policy were carried to its logical conclusion, the manufacturer would be buying everything before long, and be obliged to give up manufacturing entirely.

The illustration which I have cited is not an isolated case, but is representative of the problems faced by a large class of manufacturers. These manufacturers believe that all of the expense, however large, must be carried by the output produced, however small. This theory of expense distribution indicates a policy which in dull times would, if followed logically, put many manufacturers out of business. In 1897 the plant of which I was superintendent was put out of business by just this kind of logic. It never started up again.

Fortunately for the country, American people as a whole will finally discard theories which conflict with common sense; and, when their cost figures indicate an absurd conclusion, most of them will repudiate the figures. However, a cost system which fails us when we need it most is of but little value and it is imperative for us to devise a theory of costs that will not fail us.

Most of the cost systems in use, and the theories on which they are based, have been devised by accountants for the benefit of financiers, whose aim has been to criticize the factory and to make it responsible for all the shortcomings of the business. In this they have succeeded admirably, largely because the methods used are not so devised as to enable the superintendent to present his side of the case.

One of the prime functions of cost-keeping is to enable the superintendent to know whether or not he is doing the work he is responsible for as economically as possible, a function which is ignored in the majority of cost systems now in general use. Many accountants who make an attempt to show it are so long in getting their figures in shape that they are practically worthless for the purpose intended, the possibility of using them having passed.

In order to get a correct view of the subject we must look at the matter from a different and broader standpoint. The following illustration may put the subject in its true light:

Let us suppose that a manufacturer owns three identical plants, of an economical operating size, manufacturing the same article. One plant is located in Albany, one in Buffalo, and one in Chicago—and that they are all running at their normal capacity and are managed equally well. The amount of indirect expense per unit of product would be substantially the same in each of these factories, as would be the total cost. Now suppose business suddenly falls off to one-third of its previous amount and the manufacturer shuts down the plants in Albany and Buffalo, and continues to run the one in Chicago exactly as it has been run before. The product from the Chicago plant would have the same cost that it previously had, but the expense of carrying two idle factories might be so great as to take all the profits out of the business. In other words, the profit made from the Chicago plant might be offset entirely by the loss made by the Albany and Buffalo plants.

If these plants, instead of being in different cities, were located in the same city, a similar condition might also exist in which the expense of the two idle plants would be such a drain on the business that they would offset the profit made in the going plant.

Instead of considering these three factories to be in different parts of one city, they might be considered as being within the same yard, which would not change the conditions. Finally, we might consider that the walls between these factories were taken down and that the three factories were turned into one plant, the output of which had been reduced to one-third of its normal volume. In such case it would be manifestly proper to charge to this product only one-third of the indirect expense charged when the factory was running full.

If the above argument is correct, we may state the following general principle: THE INDIRECT EXPENSE CHARGEABLE TO THE OUTPUT OF A FACTORY SHOULD BEAR THE SAME RATIO TO THE INDIRECT EXPENSE NECESSARY TO RUN THE FACTORY AT NORMAL CAPACITY, AS THE OUTPUT IN QUESTION BEARS TO THE NORMAL OUTPUT OF THE FACTORY.

This theory of expense distribution, which was forced upon us by the abrupt change in conditions brought on by the war, explains many things which were inexplicable under the older theory. It provides the manufacturer with uniform or comparable costs as long as the methods of manufacture do not change.

Under this method of distributing expense there will be a certain amount of undistributed expense remaining whenever the factory runs below its normal capacity. A careful consideration of this item will show that it is not chargeable to the product made, but is a business expense incurred by maintaining a certain portion of the factory idle, and therefore chargeable to profit and loss. Many manufacturers have made money in a small plant only to build a large plant and lose money for years afterward, without quite understanding how it happened. This method of figuring affords an explanation and warns the manufacturer to do everything possible to increase the efficiency of the plant he has, rather than to increase its size.

This theory explains why some of our large combinations of manufacturing plants have not been as successful as was anticipated. It is also why the small plant is able to compete successfully and make money, while the combinations are only just holding their own.

The idea that money is the most powerful factor in the industrial world beginning to lose its force. It is becoming clear that the size of a business is not so important as the policy by which it is directed. If we base our policy on the idea that the cost of an article can only legitimately include the expense necessarily incurred either directly or indirectly in producing it, we shall find that our costs are much lower than we thought, and that we can do many things which under the old method of figuring appeared suicidal.

The largely held view of costs, that the product of a factory, however small, must bear the total expense, however large, is responsible for much of the confusion about costs and hence leads to unsound business policies.

If we accept the view that the article produced shall bear only that portion of the indirect expense needed to produce it, our costs will not only become lower, but relatively far more constant. The most variable factor in the cost of an article under the usual system of accounting has been the "overhead," which has varied almost inversely as the amount of the product. This item becomes substantially constant if the "overhead" is figured on the normal capacity of the plant.

Of course a method of cost-keeping does not diminish the expense, but it may show where the expense properly belongs, and give a more correct understanding of the business.

In our illustration of the three factories, the cost in the Chicago factory remained constant, but the expense of supporting the Buffalo and Albany factories in idleness was a charge against the business, and properly chargeable to profit and loss. If we had loaded this expense on the product of the Chicago factory, the cost of the product would probably have been so great as to have prevented our selling it, and the total loss would have been greater still.

When the factories are distinctly separate, few people make such a mistake, but where a single factory is three times as large as is needed for the output, the error is frequently made, with results that are just as misleading.

As a matter of fact it seems that the attempt to make a product bear the expense of that part of the plant not needed for its production is one of the most serious defects in our industrial system today. It has a farther reach than the differences between employers and employees, for if it were removed, most of those difficulties would vanish.

The problem that faces us is to find just what plant or part of a plant, is needed to produce a given output, and then to determine the "overhead" expense needed to operate that plant or portion of that plant. This is primarily the work of the manufacturer, or engineer, and only secondarily that of the accountant, who must, as far as costs are concerned, be the servant of the superintendent.

In almost all cost systems of the past the amount of "overhead" to be charged to the product, when it did not include all the "overhead," was more or less a matter of judgment. According to the theory now presented, it is not a matter of judgment, but can be determined with an accuracy depending upon the knowledge the manufacturer has of the business. Following this line of thought it should be possible for a manufacturer to calculate just what plant and equipment he ought to have, and what the staff of officers and workmen should be to turn out a given product. If this can be correctly done, the exact cost of a product can be predicted. Such a problem cannot be solved by a cost accountant without shop knowledge, but is primarily a problem for an engineer whose knowledge of materials and processes is essential for its solution.

In any attempt to solve a problem of this type, one of the most important functions we need a cost system to perform is to keep the superintendent continually advised as to how nearly he is realizing the ideal set, and to point out where the shortcomings are.

Many of us are accustomed to this viewpoint when we are treating operations singly, but few have as yet made an attempt to consider that this idea might be applied to a plant as a whole, except when the processes of manufacture are simple and the products few in number. However, when the processes become numerous or complicated, the necessity for such a check becomes more urgent, and the cost-keeper who performs this function becomes an integral part of the manufacturing system, and acts for the superintendent, as an inspector, who keeps him advised at all times of the quality of his own work.

This idea of the duties of a cost-keeper does not at all interfere with his supplying the financier with the information he needs, but insures that the information shall be correct, because the cost-keeper continually makes a comparison for the benefit of the superintendent, of what has been done with what should have been done. Costs are valuable only as comparisons, and comparisons are of little value unless we have a standard. It is the function of the engineer to set that standard.

In the past, lack of a reliable cost method has been responsible for much of the uncertainty so prevalent in our industrial policies. Now with a definite and reliable cost method that enables us to differentiate between what is lost in manufacturing and what is lost in business, it will be easy to clearly define the proper business policy.

VALUE OF AN INDUSTRIAL PROPERTY DEPENDS ON ITS PRODUCTIVE CAPACITY

I n the summer of 1916, a professor of political economy in one of our most conservative universities admitted to me that economists had been obliged to modify many of their views since the outbreak of the European war. My comment was that professors of political economy were not the only ones who had to modify their economic and industrial views.

The war taught everybody something. Although military methods have undergone radical changes, the changes in industrial methods promise to be even more radical than the military developments have been.

If there is any one thing which has been made clear by the war it is that the most important asset which either a man or nation can have is the ABILITY TO DO THINGS. Our industrial and economic developments in the past have been largely based on the theory that the most important quality a man can possess is his ability to buy things. The war has distinctly shown that this quality is secondary to the ability to do things. The recognition of this fact is having a most far-reaching effect, because it makes clear that the real assets of a nation are properly equipped industries and men trained to operate them efficiently. The money which has been spent, wisely or not, on an industrial property, and the amount of money needed to reproduce it, are both secondary in importance to the ability of that plant to accomplish the object for which it was constructed. Hence, the money spent cannot be given the first place in determining the value of the property.

Seeing that every industrial plant is built to produce some article of commerce at a cost which will enable it to compete with other producers, the value of a plant as a producing unit must depend upon its ability to accomplish the object for which it was created.

To determine the value of an industrial property, therefore, we must be able to know with accuracy the cost at which it can produce its product as well as the amount it can produce. To compare two factories on this basis their cost systems must be alike; if there is a lack of agreement as to methods of cost accounting, there will necessarily be a lack of agreement as to the estimated value of the properties. There are many methods of cost accounting; but there are only two leading theories as to what cost consists of. They are:

First, that the cost of an article must include all the expense incurred in producing it, whether such expense actually contributed to the desired end or not.

Second, that the cost of an article should include only those expenses actually needed for its production, and any other expenses incurred by the producers for any reason whatsoever must be charged to some other account.

The first theory would charge the expense of maintaining idle men and equipment to that portion of a plant not used, to the cost of the product made in that portion of the plant which was in operation. The second theory would demand that such an expense be a deduction from profits, or at least be charged to some other account. When plants are operated at their full capacity, both theories give the same cost. If, however, they are operated at less than their full capacity, the expense of carrying the idle machinery is, under the first theory, included in the cost of the product, making the cost greater. Under the second theory, this expense of idle machinery is carried in a separate account and should be deducted from the profits, leaving the cost constant. It is most interesting to note that, when costs are figured on the second basis, great activity immediately ensues to determine why machinery is idle, and to see what can be done to put it in operation. It is realized at once that this machinery had better be operated, even if no profits are obtained from its operation. Then only the expense, or even part of the expense, of owning and maintaining it is earned.

Fig. 1 illustrates this subject most clearly, and is an indication of the efficiency of management as contrasted with that of the workmen, about which we hear so much. It is interesting to note that charts of this nature, which are being made monthly in several large plants, have already had a very educational influence on the managers of those plants. They show that idle machinery which cannot be used should be disposed of, and the money received, as well as the space that it occupied, put to some useful purpose.

MILL.. Textile.................................. June,........1916....

SYMBOL	DEPARTMENT OR MACH. CLASS	% OF CAPACITY USED ON DAY TURN	TOTAL EXPENSE OF IDLENESS	DETAILS OF IDLENESS EXPENSE DUE TO					REMARKS
		10 20 30 40 50 60 70 80 90		LACK OF WORK	LACK OF HELP	LACK OF AND POOR MATERIAL	REPAIRS	POOR PLANNING	
	Spinning		18 70	18 70					
	Winding		118 74		103 74		15 00		
	Doubling		10 61	10 61					
	Twisting		17 95	17 95					
	Quilling		20 67	10 67	10 00				
	Warping		390 75			390 75			Lack of wound yarn
	Weaving		915 25	75 00		840 25			Lack of warps
	Finishing		210 72			210 72			Lack of woven goods
	Inspecting		49 70		10 70	39 00			Lack of woven goods
	Shipping		216 17	66 00		150 17			Lack of woven goods
	Total		1969 26	198 93	124 44	1630 89	15 00		

APPROVED BY _____   SUPT _____

Figure 1 Idleness Expense Chart

A little consideration of the method used in getting the data on this chart will make its value more apparent. It is a logical outgrowth of the previous chapter on Production and Costs, and is based on the fact that simple ownership of a machine costs money, inasmuch as it takes away from available assets. For instance, if we buy a machine for $1,000 we lose the interest on that $1,000, say at five per cent per year. Then, we have taxes on the machine at two per cent, and insurance of one per cent. Further, the machine probably depreciates at a rate of twenty per cent per year, and we must pay $50 or more per year for the rent of the space it occupies. All these expenses, together $330, go on whether we use the machine or not. Thus, the simple fact of our having bought this machine and kept it takes from our available assets approximately one dollar per day.

If we now ascertain the cause for idleness each day, we can find the expense of each cause of idleness as shown on the chart. That part which is due to lack of orders points out that our selling policy is wrong, or that the plant is larger than it should be — in other words, that somebody in building the plant has overestimated the demand. However, it is clear that no conclusion should be based on the figures for only one month, but on the results for a series of months during which the problem has been carefully studied. If a mistake has been made in building too large a plant, an effort should be made to determine the proper disposal or utilization of the excess, in order that the expense of idleness may be taken care of, even if no profit can be made.

The next column shows the expense due to a lack of help, which means that we must investigate the labor policy.

The next column, showing the expense due to either a lack of, or poor, material, is an indication of the efficiency of the purchasing policy and store keeping system. The next column reflects the repair and maintenance department.

If in any case the expense of idleness is greater than can be attributed to all of these causes together, it must go in the last column as poor planning.

We can hardly claim that such a chart gives us a measure of the efficiency with which the above functions are performed, but it certainly does give us an indication of that efficiency. In several cases, the first of such charts completed resulted in the scrapping of machinery which had been idle for years. The space thus saved was used for a purpose for which the superintendent had felt he needed a new building. In another case it resulted in the renting of temporarily idle machinery at a rate which went far toward covering the expense of carrying that machinery.

Under the first system of cost-keeping the facts brought out by this method are not available and the increased cost that a reduced output must bear is a great source of confusion to the salesman. The newer system with its constant cost shows that non-producing machinery is a handicap to the industry of a company, just as workmen who do not serve some useful purpose in a plant or industry, are a handicap to that plant or industry. Similarly, plants or people who do not serve some useful purpose to a community are a handicap to that community because idle plants represent idle capital, and idle people are not producers, only consumers. The warring nations recognized these facts, and put both idle plants and idle people to work wherever possible.

The statements made so far are concerned principally with the operation of industrial plants and the production of articles of commerce; but they are nonetheless true concerning the construction of industrial plants. We may ask the same question about construction that we ask about operation; for instance, should the "cost" of a railroad include all the money spent by the people engaged in building it, or should it include only such money as contributed to the building of the road? As an illustration, is the cost of a piece of road which was built and then abandoned for a superior route before being used a part of the cost of the railroad built, or is it an expense due to improper judgment on the part of the builders?

I am not discussing the question as to whether the public should be called upon to pay interest on the money uselessly spent through improper judgment, but I do think that in all construction it should be possible to separate those expenses which contributed to the desired result from those which did not. A comparison of these amounts will give a measure of the efficiency of the builders. On this knowledge, proper action can ultimately be taken.

Still another factor enters into the value of a "going plant." We all know cases where the same plant operated under one manager was a failure, yet under a different manager the plant became a very decided success. The value of a going plant, therefore, consists of two elements; namely, the value of the physical real estate and equipment, and the value of the organization operating it. In considering the value of an organization we should realize that it lies not so much in the personality of the managers or leaders (who may die or go elsewhere) as in the permanent results of their training and methods. These methods should go on with the business, and are therefore an asset and not an accident.

We have the authority of no less a person than Andrew Carnegie for the statement that his organizations were of more value to him than his plants. Before we can determine the exact value of a going plant, we must first find some means of measuring the value of the organization which operates it. This is an integral factor in the valuation of an industrial property, which is just as real as the more tangible brick and mortar of which buildings are composed.

Our charts showing the expense of idleness give us at least a rough indication of this value, for they show the expense of inefficient management.

An Extension of the Credit System to Make it Democratic

L ooking back over the great war, we have the opportunity to better understand and evaluate the different phenomena which were developed by it. Many incidents which seemed natural, and in a measure unimportant, when they took place had a profound effect upon the outcome of the war, and promise to affect still more profoundly the period to follow.

Perhaps no one incident was more significant and fraught with greater consequences to world civilization than the transfer, soon after we entered the war, of the credit center from Wall Street to Washington. This transfer took place without creating any stir, without any special opposition, and with the general approval of the community at large. We had just got the Federal Reserve Banking System into operation, and it had enormously increased our power as a nation to dispense credit. Notwithstanding the most advantageous position in which we had thus been placed, the expert financiers of Wall Street submitted without remonstrance to the transfer of the whole credit center to Washington. Compared with the "giants" of Wall Street, the men who administered from Washington were mere amateurs.

Why was it necessary for this transfer to be made, and why did Wall Street consent to it? Surely if it had been within the possibilities of Wall Street to finance the war, a serious argument would have been raised to this transfer of the credit center. The New York bankers not only did not argue, but in a most patriotic manner offered their services to help the comparatively inexperienced men in Washington handle their great undertaking.

If it had been possible for Wall Street to finance the war, it is inconceivable that the bankers of New York should have allowed the work to be taken over by other hands. Why, then, was it possible for Washington to do what was impossible for Wall Street? The answer to this question is not only very simple, but is indicative of the flaw in our entire business system. The financial methods of Wall Street were designed to operate only when we conducted "business as usual," hence their mechanism could give credit only to those who had tangible securities. They had no mechanism for extending credit to men who, although they had few or no tangible assets, might have tremendous productive capacity.

Because the war demanded that the nation as a whole produce goods to the utmost, we were obliged to invent a new kind of finance, in which the production of goods would be the first object. There was no tradition among the bankers of this country for financing any proposition except on the basis of tangible assets, and for the sole purpose of making profits. In many cases men who knew how to build ships or make guns did not have tangible assets in sufficient quantity to satisfy the usual banking system. It was therefore necessary for the Federal Government to initiate a new type of finance, at least in this country: namely, that of extending credit to a man according to his productive capacity. There was no established mechanism for doing this; it had to be done and we did it, only we did it in a rather haphazard and ineffective manner. Nevertheless, the results have justified the venture, and the possibilities of a new credit system of vastly greater potential are opening themselves to us as soon as the mechanism for its operation has been developed.

A few of the great leaders of industry have understood in a general way this kind of finance. Among them may be mentioned Mr. Andrew Carnegie, and Mr. Henry Ford. Mr. Carnegie, through an understanding of this general principle, was able to dominate the steel industry; and Mr. Ford, by the same token, became the greatest automobile manufacturer in the world. The war has backed up Mr. Carnegie and Mr. Ford by proving that productive capacity is enormously more important than wealth. Considering that our credit system has been based on "tangible assets," and not on productive capacity, there has yet to be developed an accepted mechanism for measuring the value of productive capacity.

The cost and accounting systems in general vogue take note only of what are called "tangible assets," which are necessarily static and show only potential. They make very little attempt to find out how these assets are being used. The reason undoubtedly is that they see such assets from a sales standpoint; in other words, our economic system is still patterned after the one which was originally built up to serve the needs of buying and selling. Productive capacity, on the other hand, can be measured only by taking account of what is happening. When we begin to regard matters from this standpoint, the so-called "tangible assets" are not nearly as important as the use being made of them, or the amount of product being turned out. In other words, a modern accounting system which deals with production must give us a picture of what is happening, as well as of the mechanism which causes the happenings. It must be based on charts which show what progress is taking place, and which bear the same relation to statistics as a motion picture film does to a photograph.

The question naturally asked is: If the above statements are correct, why have we not realized the correctness of them before? It took a great war, which required us to put forth all our strength, to wake us up to their importance. They have been increasing in importance for a number of years, and our failure to recognize this fact was one of the factors in producing the great catastrophe through which we have just passed.

For many years previous to the outbreak of the great war, financiers told us there couldn't be any war because the bankers wouldn't stand for it. They thought money controlled the world. Books were written to prove that we could have no more war; the idea of war was called "the great illusion." When this "illusion" was realized, they still maintained that the war could only last a few months. Nevertheless it lasted over four years, to the great confusion of our economists and theorists. We all know now that it was not supported by finance, but by the grand scale production of modern industry. It stopped not for lack of money, but for lack of means to live and fight with. We see then, without any shadow of a doubt, that inasmuch as production was the controlling factor in the great war, it will hereafter be the controlling factor in the world. Whichever nation first recognizes the fundamental fact *that production and not money* must be the aim of our economic system, will exert a predominating influence on the civilization, which is to be built up in the period of reconstruction that we are now entering.

Our immediate problem is to develop a credit system that will enable us to take advantage of all the productive forces in the community. Such a credit system must not only be able to finance those who have ownership, but also those who have productive capacity, which is vastly more important. This is equivalent to saying that *our wealth in men is more important than our wealth in materials.* So far we have never used this force to more than a small fraction of its capacity, simply for the reason that the originators of our financial system were traders and not producers. Now, however, when the supreme importance of the producer has been recognized, we must enlarge our credit system to enable us to take full advantage of his possibilities; in other words, we must make it democratic.

To meet the difficulties of war, the Federal Government had no hesitation in inaugurating such a finance for the benefit of the community. While it was done in a new and crude manner, we recognize that it was in the main successful. We will soon find that there are difficulties in times of peace as well that could be helped by a similar financial method. Some nations are going to see this, and realizing that the credit system of the country must always be available for the benefit of the community, take such action as to accomplish that result, thereby forcing others to do the same. Through the War Finance Corporation Act (amended) section 21, March 3, 1919, we have already taken such action with regard to exports. During the war, we financed necessary production with public money; now in time of peace we finance another essential activity with public money. This is a most encouraging beginning. Can we not make public money available to finance all socially necessary activities whether in time of war or peace?

In the past what a man could do was limited by his financial and social condition; hence many of our most capable men were severely restricted in their activities. To be sure, there have been a few who have been able to rise above their restrictions—a rail-splitter becomes the president of a great republic, and a harness-maker the first president of another*. However, these examples only illustrate the possibilities that are under-utilized, because our credit system has not been democratic.

*Gannt refers here to Abraham Lincoln, a rail-splitter who went on to become the 16th President of the United States, and of Friedrich Ebert, a saddle-maker turned Social Democrat, who was chosen as the first president of the new German Republic.

Economics of Democracy

The prime function of a science is to better enable us to anticipate the future in the field with which it concerns itself. Judged by this standard, economic science has been practically worthless. It has absolutely failed to warn us of the greatest catastrophe that has ever befallen the civilized world. In addition when the catastrophe burst upon us, economists and financiers persisted in belittling it by insisting that the great war could last only a few months. Are they any nearer the truth in their theories of labor and capital, protection and free trade, or taxation?

When they talk about preparedness, what do they mean? *Do they mean that we must order our living as to prevent another such catastrophe, or do they simply mean that we must aim to be strong when the next catastrophe comes?*

The latest economic thought indicates that the fundamentals of both kinds of preparedness are the same, and that preparation for the former is the best basis on which to establish preparation for the latter. *True preparedness, then, would seem to consist in a readjustment of our economic conditions with the object of averting another such catastrophe.*

In considering this subject we must realize that:

The Nation reflects its leaders.

The Army reflects its general.

The Factory reflects its manager.

In a successful industrial nation, the industrial leaders must ultimately become the leaders of the nation. The condition of the industries will then become a true index of the condition of the nation. If the industries are not properly managed for the benefit of the whole community, no amount of *military* preparedness will avail in a real *war*. The military preparations of Germany, vast as they were, would have collapsed in six months had it not been for the social and industrial conditions on which they were based.

Army officers and others have told us most emphatically what military preparedness is, and how to get it. Innumerable papers have been written on industrial preparedness, and people in general are getting a pretty clear idea of what we mean by the term. Moreover, many are beginning to appreciate our lack in this respect. Figures 2, 3, 4, and 5 illustrate what this means.

Admittedly these pictures are not typical of our industries, but they do represent a condition which is all too common. These conditions must be corrected if we are to be prepared for either peace or war.

Our record in the production of munitions, especially of ammunition, is not one to be proud of. Note what Mr. Bascom Little, President of the Cleveland, Ohio, Chamber of Commerce, and Chairman of the National Defense Committee of the Chamber of Commerce of the United States, said in the spring of 1916:

> "The work of Mr. Coffin's committee has seemed to us very important, and so clearly related, in such practical ways, to what the business organizations of the country are trying to do to further national defense, that those with which I am connected immediately formed a union with the committee on learning of its work.
>
> The thing that has stirred up the business men of the Mid-West during the past eighteen months has been the lesson they have learned in the making of war materials. It points a very vivid moral to all our people. It all looked very easy when it started a year and a half ago. The plant with which I am associated in Cleveland got an order for 250,000 three-inch high explosive shells. It was a simple enough looking job—just a question of machining. The forgings were shipped to us and we were to finish and deliver. It began to dawn on us when the forgings came, that this order that looked so big to us, was less than one day's supply of shells for France or England or Russia; and we felt that in eight months by turning our plant, which is a first-class machine shop, onto this job we could fill the order. In a little while we got up against the process of hardening. That—and mark what I say—was fourteen months ago. To date we

have shipped and had accepted 130,000 shells, of which a full half are not complete. They still have to be fitted by the fuse maker, then fitted in the brass cartridge cases with the propelling charge, and somewhere, sometime, maybe, they will get on the battlefield of Europe. Up to the present, none of them has arrived there.

"Now this is the situation in a high-class efficient American plant. This is what happened when it turned to making munitions of war. The same thing has occurred in so many Middle Western plants, that their owners have made up their minds that if they are ever going to be called upon for service to their own country, they must know more about this business. They feel that they are now liabilities to the nation, and not assets in case of war. *Proud as we may be of our industrial perfection, it has not worked here, and the country — particularly you in the East — may as well know it.*"

FIG. 2. — UNPREPARED

FIG. 3. — PREPARED

Two views of the same shop doing substantially the same work. The lower picture was taken about a year after the upper from a slightly different viewpoint.

FIG. 4. — UNPREPARED

FIG. 5. — PREPARED

Two views of the same shop doing substantially the same work, taken from the same point. The lower view was taken about a year after the upper.

The criticism on this will be that it is three years old, and that we have made great advances since then. In reply I can only say that if we have made marked advances I have been utterly unable to discover them.

Even a casual investigation into the reasons why so many of the munitions manufacturers have not made good, reveals the fact that *their failure is due to lack of managerial ability* rather than to any other cause. Without efficiency in management, efficiency of the workmen is useless, even if it is possible to get it. With efficient management there is little difficulty in training the workmen to be efficient. I have proved this so many times and so clearly that there can be no doubt about it. *Our most serious trouble is incompetence in high places.* As long as that remains uncorrected, no amount of efficiency in the workmen will avail very much.

The pictures by which this chapter is illustrated do not show anything concerning the efficiency of the individual workman. They are a sweeping condemnation of the inefficiency of those responsible for the management. These pictures illustrate the fact, so well known to many of us, that our industries are suffering from lack competent managers. In other words, it seems as if many of those who control our industries hold their positions, not through their ability to accomplish results, but for some other reason. Industrial control is too often based on favoritism or privilege, rather than on ability. *This hampers the healthy, normal development of industrialism, which can reach its highest development only when equal opportunity is secured to all, and when all reward is equitably proportioned to service rendered. In other words, when industry becomes democratic.*

Therefore, we are brought face to face with a form of preparedness which is even more fundamental than the Industrial Preparedness usually referred to, and I am indebted to Mr. W. N. Polakov for the name "Social Preparedness." Social Preparedness means the democratization of industry and the establishment of such relations among citizens themselves as well as the citizens and the government. Establishing such a relationship will cause a hearty and spontaneous response on the part of the citizenry to the needs of the country.

At the great war broke out and spread over Europe, the thing which perhaps surprised us most was the enthusiasm with which the German people entered into warfare. Hardly less striking was the slowness with which the rank and file of Englishmen realized the problems they were up against, and their responsibilities concerning them.

A short consideration of what happened in Germany in the last half of the nineteenth century, may throw some light on this subject. Bismarck and Von Moltke, following the lead of Frederick the Great, believed and taught that the great industry of a country was War. In other words, that it was more profitable to take by violence from another than to produce. The history of the world, *until the development of modern industrialism*, seemed to bear out that theory. Bismarck argued that to be strong from a military standpoint the nation must have a large number of well trained, intelligent, and healthy men, and he set about so ordering the industries of Germany as to produce that result.

Military autocracy forced business and industry to see that men were properly trained and that their health was safe-guarded. In other words, because of the necessity of the military state for such men, the state saw to it that industry was so organized as to develop high-grade men. The result being that a kind of industrial democracy was developed under the paternalistic guidance of an autocratic military party.

Under such influences, the increase of education and the development of men went on apace, and were soon reflected in an industrial system which was on track to surpass any other in the world.

In England, on the other hand, the business system was

controlled by an autocratic and "socially irresponsible finance," which, to a large extent, disregarded the interest of the workman and of the community. At the breaking out of war, the superiority of German industries over the industries of England was manifest, not only by the feeling of the people, but by their loyalty to the National Government, which had so cared for, or disregarded, their individual welfare. This superiority became so rapidly apparent, that in order to make any headway against Germany, England was obliged to imitate the methods which had been developed in Germany. In doing so, England had to say that *the industries* (particularly the munitions factories) *which were needed for the salvation of the country, must serve the country and not the individual.* The increased efficiency which England showed after the adoption of this method was most marked, and in striking contrast with the inefficiency displayed previously in similar work.

Our industries are managed in the interest of an autocratic financial system and not in the interest of the community. In Germany it was proved beyond doubt that when an industrial system is forced by military autocracy to serve the community, it is vastly stronger than an industrial system which serves only a financial autocracy.

The method by which Germany developed a single mindedness of purpose that carried the tremendous power of both war and peace—namely, autocratic military authority—is hateful to us. That being said, we must not lose sight of the fact that such power was developed and may be developed by some other nation again in the future. If we are to be strong when again faced with a contingency of developing a greater strength, or submitting, we must first of all develop a singleness of purpose for the whole community.

England demonstrated the same thing; if England had not rapidly increased her efficiency in the production of munitions, it would have been a sad day for the British Empire.

In considering these facts, we should ask ourselves if there is not some fundamental fact which is accountable for the success of industry under such control. The one thing which stands out most prominently is the fact that, in the attempt to make the industries serve the community, *an attempt was made to abolish industrial privilege, and to give every man an opportunity to do what he could and thereby reward him accordingly.*

As stated before, the industrial system of Germany was developed largely as an adjunct to its military system. Yet it was this system, to a degree at least, that forced the abolition of financial and industrial privilege, and thereby in a large measure eliminated incompetence in high places. What results could we expect if we abolished privilege absolutely, and devoted all our efforts to the development of an industrialism which would serve the community and thus "develop the unconquerable power of real democracy?"

The close of the war and the abolition of political autocracy has brought us face to face with the question of making a choice between the economic autocracy of the past, or an economic democracy. To prove that this is not mere idle speculation, note what one of our leading financiers said on the subject during the war:

> "The President of the New York Life Insurance Company," says Mr. Charles Ferguson, "told the State Chamber of Commerce, during the great war, that under modern conditions the existence of even two rival sovereignties on this little planet has become absurd. This is true. We must therefore drive forward, through incredible waste and slaughter, to settle the question of which of the rival Powers is to build the New Rome and establish a military world-state on the Cesarean model — or else we must now set our faces toward a real democracy."

What is the basis of such a democracy?

Like the Catholic Church of the middle ages, the one thing which crosses all frontiers and binds all people together, is business. The Chinese and the American, by means of an interpreter, find a common interest in business. Business is therefore the one possible bond which may bring universal peace. *Economists and financiers fully realized this, and believed that an autocratic finance could accomplish the result.* That was their fatal error. *The beneficiaries of privilege invariably battle among themselves, even if they are strong enough to hold in subjection those that have no privileges, and who have to bear the brunt of the fight.*

This is true whether the beneficiaries are individuals or nations. Hence neither internal strife nor external war can be eliminated as long as some people have privileges over others.

If privilege is eliminated, not only will the danger of war be minimized, but the causes of domestic strife will also reduce in number. Then, and not until then, will the human race be in a position to make a continuous and uninterrupted advance.

The nation which first realizes this fact and eliminates privilege from business will have a distinct lead on all others. All other conditions being equal, that nation will rapidly rise to a dominating place in the world. Such a nation will do by the arts of peace, that which some Germans seemed to think was their mission to do by means of war. The opportunity is knocking at our door. Shall we turn it away?

The answer is that we must not turn it away. In fact, we dare not, if we would escape the economic convulsion that is now spreading over Europe. Soon after the signing of the armistice, Mr. David R. Francis, former ambassador to Russia, said that the object of the Soviet Government was to prevent the exploitation of one man by another. According to Mr. Francis, the cause of this convulsion is the attempt of the social body to free itself of the exploitation of one man by another. Then he added, "Such an aim is manifestly absurd."

The convulsion is made all the more severe because there are people in every community that not only consider this aim absurd, but use all their influence to prevent the accomplishment of it.

When, at the end of a victorious war for democracy, a prominent representative of the victors is willing to proclaim publicly such a sentiment, it is perfectly evident that we have not yet solved all of our problems. Whether we approve of the Soviet method of government or not, even Mr. Francis must admit that their aim, as expressed by him, is a worthy one. It would be surprising if, in the time which has elapsed since the Russian revolution, an entirely satisfactory and permanent method should have been developed to prevent the exploitation of one man by another. The fact that they have not yet established such a government is hardly a basis for the statement that such a government is absurd.

This statement by Mr. Francis brings to the front the question — Is the business system of our future going to continue to be one of exploitation of one man by another, or is it possible to have a business system from which such privilege has been eliminated?

In this connection it may be interesting to note that for the past fifteen years, I and a small band of co-workers, have been attempting to develop a system of industrial management which should not be dependent on the exploitation of one man by another, but should aim to give each as nearly as possible his just dues. Strange as it may seem to those of the old way of thinking, the more nearly successful we have been in this attempt, the more prosperous have the concerns adopting our methods become. In view of this fact we beg to submit that the proposition does not seem to us to be absurd, even though we may not admit that any of the solutions heretofore offered have really accomplished the result. In a subsequent chapter, however, we shall present the progress which we have recently made in this direction.

DEMOCRACY IN PRODUCTION
(PROGRESS CHARTS)

I t is a common perception that the offensive strategy devised by General Foch* after the Germans missed a strategic opportunity of crushing his forces between Montdidier and Chateau-Thierry, would have ended the war.

---

*Ferdinand Foch was the French Supreme Commander of the allied armies. He engineered the *Grand Offensive* which resulted in the defeat of the Germans. At the signing of the Treaty of Versailles, he said "This is not a peace, it is a twenty year armistice." His prediction proved to be devastatingly accurate.

The infusion of morale, generated by the arrival of American troops, would have quickly carried the French to victory even if the Germans been able to economically sustain their war machine, or maintain their national desire to fight. However, it is a fact that a growing discontent due to the increasing hardships which their economic system was unable to relieve, and which threatened a revolution, was unquestionably an important factor in lowering the morale of the army and worked strongly in our favor. Of course, knowledge of the real conditions at home was kept as far as possible from the soldiers at the front, but from what we have learned since the armistice, it must have been perfectly clear to those in control some time before the armistice, that their economic strength was exhausted, and the end had come.

It has been suggested that the attempt of the Germans to extend the salient at Château Thierry before flattening out the salient between Montdidier, was taking a "gambler's chance," for they realized then that they were near the end of their economic resources and that victory must come quick or not at all.

Whether this theory is true or not, the fact remains that the threatened collapse of the economic system was a controlling factor during the last few months of the war. In other words, war cannot be waged unless the economic system is capable of supporting the population as well as furnishing the machines of warfare. Therefore, to be as strong as possible in war, we must develop an economic system which will enable us to exert all our strength for the common good, which will therefore be free from autocratic practices of either rich or poor, for such practices take away from the community for the benefit of a class.

It is generally agreed that this philosophy is correct in time of war, but both the rich and the poor seem to think that we do not need to be strong in time of peace, and that we may with impunity go back to the pull and haul for profits regardless of the results to the community. Such a condition does not produce strength and harmony, but weakness and discord.

In the struggle that arises under the above conditions, between an autocratic ownership and an autocratic labor party, the economic laws which produce national strength are largely disregarded. From that point the whole industrial and business system becomes infected with such a feebleness that it is incapable of supporting our complicated system of modern civilization. This is exactly what is happening in eastern Europe, where civilization is tottering due to the fact that the industrial and business system by which it was supported, is no longer functioning properly. The production portion seems to have broken down, hence there is a shortage everywhere of the necessities of life. This failure is undoubtedly due to a combination of causes; but whatever the cause, the result is the same. The violation of economic laws, whether through interest, ignorance, or indolence, will ultimately, to use the language of a distinguished economist, "blow the roof off our civilization just as surely as the violation of the laws of chemistry will produce an explosion in the laboratory."

We must avoid the possibility of this explosion at all hazards. For us to accomplish this result we must begin at once, not only to make clear what the correct economic laws are, but to take such steps in conformity with them as will get the support of the community in general. Doing so will lessen the danger of our following Europe into the chaos toward which she seems heading.

Those who believed the war could last only a few months based their opinion on the destruction of wealth it would cause. They had absolutely no conception of the tremendous speed with which this loss might be made good by the productive force of modern industry. They did not understand that the controlling factor in the war would ultimately become *productive capacity.*

When we entered the war, it was of course necessary to raise money, and through the persistent use of the slogan

"Money will win the war", our loans were promptly oversubscribed. Although we were able to raise all the money we needed, we had difficulty in transforming that money quickly into fighting power. We made the fundamental error of considering that those who knew how to raise money also knew how to transform it into food, clothing, weapons, and ships. The sudden end of the war prevented us from realizing how great this error was. Even a superficial review of what took place during 1918 reveals the fact that our efforts at production were sadly ineffective. This is so true that some of those in authority not only discouraged all efforts to show comparison between their promises and their performances, but they actually forbade such comparisons to be made.

At the beginning of the war there was one man in Washington who understood the necessity for just this kind of record, which should be kept from day to day and should show our progress in the work we had to do. This man was Brigadier General William Crozier, Chief of Ordnance. Apparently alone among those in authority at that time, he recognized the important principle that *authority and responsibility for performance must be centered in the same individual, and organized his department on that basis.* Before war broke out, a simple chart system, which showed the comparison between promises and performances, had been established in the Frankford Arsenal. General Crozier began to extend this system throughout the Ordnance Department as soon as we entered the war in order to see how each of his subordinates was performing the work assigned to him. As the method was new, progress was necessarily slow, but before General Crozier was removed from his position as Chief of Ordnance, in December, 1917, a majority of the activities of the Ordnance Department were shown in chart form so clearly that progress, *or lack of progress,* could be seen at once. No other government department at the time had so clear a picture of its problems and the progress being made in handling them.

The following incident will serve to show the results that

had been produced by this policy. Late in November, 1917, Dean Herman Schneider of the University of Cincinnati, was called to the Ordnance Department to assist on the labor problem. Before deciding just how he would attack his problem, he naturally investigated the activities of the department as a whole. He reported his findings in December, 1917, in a letter he wrote to General C. B. Wheeler. The following is an extract of that letter:

"The number of men needed for the Ordnance Program should be ascertained in the production sections of the several divisions of the Ordnance Department. Investigation so far (in three production sections) discloses that, except in isolated cases, a shortage of labor is not evident.'

"Each production section had production and progress chart systems. These seem to vary in minor details only. Even without rigid standardization, the charts give a picture of the progress of the whole Ordnance Program, including lags and the causes for them. Combined in one office and kept to date they would show the requirements as to workers, as well as to materials, transportation, accessory machinery, and all of the other factors which make or break the program.

"With a plan of this sort the Ordnance Department would be in a position to state *at any time its immediate and probable future needs in men, materials, transportation, and equipment.*

"The other Departments of the War Department (and of other departments engaged in obtaining war material) can, through their Production Sections, do what the Ordnance Department has done; assemble in central offices their production and progress charts through which they would know their immediate and probable future needs.

"Finally, these charts assembled in one clearing office would give the data necessary in order *to make the
whole program of war production move with fair uniformity,
without disastrous competition and with justice to the workers.*"

This letter not only clearly sets forth what General Crozier had accomplished, but it shows still more clearly Dean
Schneider's conception of the problem which at that time lay
before us. General Crozier's successors allowed the methods
which had been developed to lapse, and Dean Schneider's vision of the industrial problem and ability to handle it were
relegated to second place.

The methods referred to by Dean Schneider were afterward adopted in an elementary way by the Shipping Board
and by the Emergency Fleet Corporation. Although they were
never used to any great extent by those in highest authority,
who apparently were satisfied to report what they had done,
rather than to compare it too closely with what they might
have done, they were used to great advantage by many who
were responsible for results in detail.

Fig. 6 is a sample of the charts referred to above. This is
an actual Ordnance Department chart, entered up to the end
of December 1917, the names of the items being replaced by
letters. It was used to illustrate the methods employed and to
instruct people in the work.

The distance between the current date and the end of the
heavy or cumulative line indicates whether the deliveries of
any article are ahead or behind schedule and by how much. It
is thus seen that the short lines indicate instantly the articles
which need attention.

As said before, when General Crozier was moved from his
office about the 1st of December 1917, he had a majority of the
items for which he was responsible charted in this manner
and was rapidly getting the same kind of knowledge about

the other items. Charts of this character were on his desk at all times and he made constant use of them.

This chart is shown only as a sample and represents a principle. Each item on such a chart may have been purchased from a dozen different suppliers, in which case the man responsible for procuring such articles had the schedule and progress of each contract charted in a manner similar to that on Chart 6. Chart 7 is such a chart. The lines on Chart 6 represented a summary of all the lines on corresponding detail charts.

Similar charts were used during the war show the schedules and progress in building ships, shipyards, and flying boats—and are now being used for the same purpose in connect with the manufacture of many kinds of machinery. The great advantage of this type of chart, known as the straight line chart, is that it enables us to make a large number of comparisons at once.

ARTICLES	TOTAL AMOUNT ORDERED	1917 January	February	March	April	May	June	July	August	Sept.	Oct.	Nov.	Entered to December 31, st 1917 Dec.
A	664,632	10M	11M 21M	32M	43M 16M	58M 37M	96M 22M	118M 118M 20M-Z	138M	52M 190M 157M	347M 257M	604M 39M	643M
B	142,004	618-Z	2618 3M 3618	7M 3M	10M 4M	14M	18M 11M	29M	40M 21M	61M 22M	83M 26M	109M 23M	132M
C	156,670			18-Z	0-Z	16	0-Z	2M 2M-Z	4M-7M	11M 22M	33M 34M	67M 34M	101M
D	4,000	250-Z	500	750	1000 252-Z	1252 1252	0-Z	0-Z	0-Z	2125 873-Z	2750 625	3375	4000

FIGURE 6 PROGRESS CHART

At the left of figure 6 is a list of articles to be procured. The amounts for which the orders have been placed are shown in the column headed "Amount Ordered." The dates between deliveries are shown by right angles. The amount to be delivered each month is shown by a figure at the left side of the space assigned to that month. The figure at the right of each time space shows the total amount to be delivered up to that date. If the amount due in any month is all received, a light line is drawn clear across that month. If only half the amount due is received, a light line is drawn across that month. In general, the length of the light line or the number of lines indicates the amount delivered during that month. The heavy line shows cumulatively the amount delivered up to the date of the last entry. It will be noted that, if this line is drawn to the scale of the periods through which it passes, the distance from the end of the line to the current date will represent the amount of time deliveries are behind or ahead of schedule. The short cumulative lines are the ones that need attention, as they represent items that are farthest behind schedule. Z represents no deliveries.

64

Entered to December 31st, 1917

CONTRACTOR	ORDER NUMBER	TOTAL AMOUNT ORDERED	January	February	March	April	May	June	July	August	Sept.	Oct.	Nov.	Dec.
A		664,632	10M	11M 21M	32M	43M 16M	58M 37M	96M 22M	118M	138M 20M	52M 190M	157M 347M	257M 604M	39M 643M
	6228	57,000	9500											2
2	6254	8,120					4060	N	N	N	21504	N		
3	6562	22,000						2200	N					
4	EE24	25,000						22M	18M		5M 5M	10M 5M N	10000	3000
5	6505	81,000								N		5M N		25M
6	EE45	100,000									25M N	38M	37M	N
7	EE59	225,000										100M	105M N	10M N
8	6292	131,512		1250							522			
9	6298	5,000					3323							
10	6391	10,000												

FIGURE 7 ORDER CHART

The top line on figure 7 is a summary of the individual orders and is represented in the figure 6 chart by line A.

From the illustrations given the following principles upon which this chart system is founded are easily comprehended:

First: The fact that all activities can be measured by the amount of time needed to perform them.

Second: The space representing the time unit on the chart can be made to represent the amount of activity which should have taken place in that time.

Bearing in mind these two principles, the whole system is readily intelligible and affords a means of charting all kinds of activities, the common measure being time.

Democracy in the Shop
(Man Records)

I n the chapter titled "An Extension of the Credit System," we referred only to financial credit. Of course, the term credit has a much broader meaning. For instance, when a man has proved his knowledge on a certain subject, we "give him credit" for that knowledge; when he has proved his ability to do things, we "give him credit" for that ability. In other words, we have confidence that he will make good. The credit which we give a man, or the confidence which we place in him, is usually based on his record. We placed confidence in General Pershing because of his record. We gave him credit for being able to handle the biggest job we had and our faith was not misplaced. If we had an exact record of the doings of every man, we should have a very comprehensive guide for the placing of confidence and the extending of credit—even financial credit.

However, as our record of individuals is exceedingly meager and our information concerning them is usually derived from interested parties, we have very little substantial basis for placing confidence in, or extending credit to, people in general. It is hardly to be expected that a business system will risk investment without a more substantial guarantee for the financial credit it extends. It would seem that if we really wish to establish such a credit system as is described in Chapter VI, we must keep such a record of the activities of individuals as will furnish the information needed to give a proper guarantee.

Be that as it may, all records are comparative, and the record of a man's performance is comparatively valueless unless we are able to compare what he has done with what he should have done. The possibilities in the modern industrial system are so great that there is scarcely any idea of them by people in general. In fact, many accomplishments which have been heralded as quite extraordinary are shown, on careful examination, to have been quite the reverse, when a comparison is made with the possibilities.

In the past if a man has accomplished a desirable result, we have been apt to let it go on its face value, and have seldom inquired into how it was done. We have no criticism of this as a habit of the past, but the war has brought an entirely different viewpoint into the world. Besides we Americans, it has shown others how inefficient the world is in conducting its civilization. Other peoples have realized that the real asset of a nation is its human power, and undoubtedly will soon begin to adopt means of measuring this power to the end that they may use it more effectively.

Some of us have made a start in this work by keeping individual records of operatives, showing as nearly as possible what they have done in comparison with what they might have done, with the reasons for their failing to accomplish the full amount. By systematically attempting to remove the obstacles which stood in the way of complete accomplishment, we have secured a remarkable degree of co-operation and developed possibilities in workmen which, until now, had been unsuspected. Further, we have developed the fact that nearly all workers welcome any assistance which may be given them by the foreman in removing the obstacles which confront them, and teaching them to become better workers. Chart No. 8 is an actual chart of this type from a factory and covers a period of two weeks. Each working day was ten hours, except Saturday, which was five. The charts are ruled accordingly. If a worker did all that was expected of him in a day the thin line goes clear across the space representing that day, and if he did more or less, the number of such thin lines or the length of the line indicate the amount. The number of days' work he did in a week is represented by the heavy line. Wherever a dotted line is shown, it indicates that during that time the man worked on a job for which we had no estimated time. The letters are symbols indicating the cause of failure to perform the full amount of work. A key to these symbols follows Chart No. 8.

According to our idea of management, it is a foreman's function to remove the obstacles confronting the workmen and to teach them how to do their work. An average of the performance of the workmen is a very fair measure of the efficiency of the foreman; this is shown by the line at the top of the chart. It can readily be seen that such a chart system gives a very fair means of fixing the compensation of workers and foremen. A series of such charts, kept up week after week, will give us a measure of the amount of confidence which we may place in the individual foreman and workman, for if all obstacles are removed by the foreman, the workman's line is a measure of his effectiveness.

Just as the line representing the average of all the workers is a measure of the foreman, so a line representing the average of the foremen is in some degree a measure of the superintendent.

The improvement which has been made by workers under our teaching and record–keeping systems involves more than is at first apparent. For instance, it has clearly been proven that poor workmen are much more apt to migrate than good workmen. The natural conclusion from this is that if we wish to make workmen permanent, our first step must be to make better workmen of them. Our experience proves the conclusion to be correct.

Many of our large industrial concerns estimated that the cost of breaking in a new employee is very high—running from about $35.00 up (In 2006 dollars that equals $5,895.76*). We have already satisfied ourselves that if only a fraction of this amount is expended in training the inferior workman, we can reduce migration drastically. In other words, money spent in proper teaching and training of workmen is a highly profitable investment for any industrial concern, provided there is some means of measuring and recording the result. So beneficial have our methods proved that we are inclined to believe that *the practice of stealing good workmen from one's competitor will ultimately prove to be as unprofitable as stealing his property.*

---

*Williamson, Samuel H. "Five Ways to Compute the Relative Wealth of a U.S. Dollar Amount, 1790-2006," MeasuringWorth.com, 2007.

Man _ _ _ **RECORD CHART FOR** _ _ _ **DEPT.**

NAME	NO		Mon.3	Tues.4	Wed.5	Thurs.6	Fri.7	Sat.8	Mon.10	Tues.11	Wed.12	Thurs.13	Fri.14	Sat.15
PALEN				64%		5%A	28%			72%			28%	
Griffen	501		T		T		T		T	T	T	T	T	T
Palen	503		G	G	G	G	G		G	G	T	I	G	
Millpaugh	507			T										
Owens	514					A	A	A						
Rogee	517													
Williams	519		T		I	T		T	T	T	T	I		
Martell	527						I							T
Stewart	535		G	G	G	G		G	G	G	G	G		

	The daily space represents the amount of work a man should have done in a day, and also the time taken to do the work.
	Estimated time for work done.
⸺	Cumulative estimated time for work done.
-------	Total time used on work not estimated.
-------	Unestimated time on job.

Legend

A: Absent	I: Lack of instruction	V: Holiday	D: Defective work	X: Reason not clear
G: Green operator	T: Tool troubles, or lack of tools			M: Lack of or defective material

FIGURE 8A KEY FOR MAN RECORD CHART

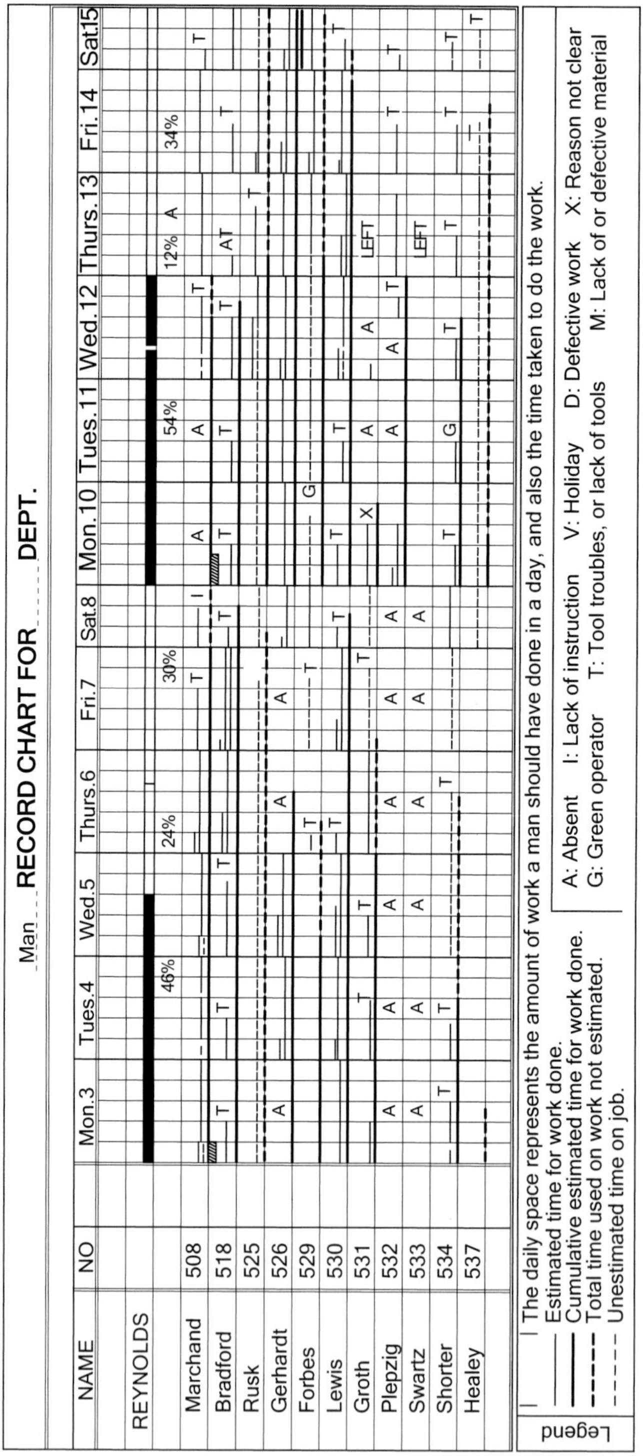

Man ____ RECORD CHART FOR ____ DEPT.

NAME	NO	Mon.3	Tues.4	Wed.5	Thurs.6	Fri.7	Sat.8	Mon.10	Tues.11	Wed.12	Thurs.13	Fri.14	Sat.15
REYNOLDS													
Marchand	508		46%		24%	30%			54%		12% A	34%	
Bradford	518	T	T			T	I	A	A	T	A		T
Rusk	525			T			T	T	T	T	AT	T	
Gerhardt	526	A			A	A					T		
Forbes	529							G					
Lewis	530				T	T	T	T	T	T		T	T
Groth	531		T	T				X	A	A	LEFT		T
Plepzig	532	A	A	A	A	A	A		A	A		T	T
Swartz	533	A	A	A	A	A	A			A	LEFT		
Shorter	534	T	T		T			T	G	T	T	T	T
Healey	537												T

Legend

| The daily space represents the amount of work a man should have done in a day, and also the time taken to do the work. |
— Estimated time for work done.
—— Cumulative estimated time for work done.
– – – Total time used on work not estimated.
- - - - Unestimated time on job.

A: Absent   I: Lack of instruction   V: Holiday   X: Reason not clear
G: Green operator   T: Tool troubles, or lack of tools   D: Defective work   M: Lack of or defective material

FIGURE 8B KEY FOR MAN RECORD CHART

Before the rise of modern industry the world was controlled largely by predatory nations who held their own by exploiting and taking by force of arms from their less powerful neighbors. With the rise of modern industrialism, productive capacity has been proven so much stronger than military power that we believe the last grand scale attempt to practice the latter method of attaining wealth or power has been made. In this great war it was clearly proven that it is not what we *have* but what we can *do* which is more important. It clearly follows then that the workers we have are not so important as our ability to train others; again illustrating the fact that our productive capacity is more important than our possessions.

The fact that the methods which I have so inadequately described are of broad applicability, has been proven by the fact that they have received enthusiastic support of workmen wherever they have been tried. As previously said, it is undoubtedly true that the "efficiency" methods which have been in vogue for the past twenty years in this country have failed to produce what was expected of them. The reason seems to be that we have to a large extent ignored the human factor and failed to take advantage of the ability and desire of the ordinary man to *learn and to improve his position*. Furthermore, these "efficiency" methods have been applied in a manner that was highly autocratic. This alone would be sufficient to condemn them, even if they had been highly effective, which they have not.

In this connection it has clearly been proven that better results can be accomplished if the man who trains the workman also inspects the work. This way, he not only shows the workman where he is wrong, but how to correct his errors. The attempt to combine instruction and inspection in one man has met with the highest approval among the workmen, with the result of better work and less loss. This method is contrary to the usual practice, inasmuch as instruction and inspection have been considered two functions, the former requiring an expert and the latter a much less capable, and hence cheaper, man. We are satisfied that this analysis is defective; the inspector who can show the workman how to avoid his errors is usually worth far more than the extra compensation required to secure his services. It may be impossible to measure the exact material value of these methods individually, but the total effect is reflected in an improved and increased product at a lower cost.

Seeing that it is not necessary for any coercion in applying these methods when we have an instructor who is capable of being a leader, we rapidly attain a high degree of democracy in the shop. On the other hand, if the chosen instructor fails to measure up to the standard of leadership, it is never long before his shortcomings are exposed, for through the medium of our charts available facts are easily comprehended by all. By these methods we automatically select as leader the man who knows what to do and how to do it. When he has been found and installed, progress is rapid and sure.

Democracy in Management
(Machine Records)

Having demonstrated by experience that it is possible to run a shop democratically and that the idea of giving every man a fair show and rewarding him accordingly thing but absurd, we naturally ask how far upward into the management we can carry this principle. The world still believes that authority must be conferred, and has a very faint conception of what we mean by *intrinsic authority*, or the authority that comes to a man who knows what to do and how to do it, and who is not so much concerned with being followed as on getting ahead.

The problem of the manager is much wider than that of the superintendent or the foreman, for he must see that there is work to be done, materials to work with, and men to do the work. These duties, as well as numerous others, are not within the sphere of the foreman.

The object of a shop being to produce goods, the first problem which comes to the manager is to find out to what extent the shop is performing the function for which it was built. In other words, are the various production machines operating all the time and if not, why not? An opportunity for our chart comes in again, and the reason why a machine did not work at all is indicated by symbols. Chart No. 9 is one of this type. The thin lines represent the number of hours each day a machine was operated; the heavy line represents the total number of hours it operated during the week. The symbols indicate the causes of idleness; some were due to lack of work; some to lack of material; some to lack of men; others still on account of repairs, etc. If we do not have enough work to keep the shop busy, we must look for the cause by asking: Is there work to be had? Is our price low enough? Is our quality good enough? The answer to the first two must be determined by the manager in connection with the sales department. The third by the manager in connection with the shop superintendent. If our idleness is due to lack of material, the question must be taken up with the buyer and storekeeper. If it is due to lack of help, the labor policy and the wage system must be studied. If the idleness is due to repairs on machinery, the question is one for consideration by the superintendent and the maintenance department. In every case the responsibility for a condition is traced directly to its source. Moreover, as it is entirely possible to determine the expense incurred by idleness, such expense may be allocated directly to the responsible parties.

Considering that a real management system is simply a

mechanism for keeping all concerned fully advised as to the needs of a shop, and showing continuously how these needs have been supplied. *The comparison between what each man from the top to the bottom did and what he should have done* is easily made. Under a system of management based on our charts, it soon becomes evident to everyone who is performing his function properly and who is not. A man who is not making a success knows about it as soon as anybody else and has the opportunity of doing better if he can. If he is not making good, it is very seldom that he has any desire to hold on to the job and advertise his incompetence to his fellows. Likewise, it takes only limited experience with these methods to convince a man that his record will discredit him very much if he uses opinions instead of facts in determining his methods and policies. Along these lines we are able to apply the same standards to those in authority that we apply to the workmen. In other words we ask of all — how well did he perform his task? A short line on a chart points unfailingly to him who needs the most help.

The Machine Record charts just referred to have to do with what proportion of the plant was operated. The Man Record charts indicate the effectiveness with which the machines were operated during the time they were operated. For instance, if a machine was operated only one-half the time, and with only one-half of its effectiveness during that time, we would only get one quarter of possible use from the machine. A combination of these two sets of charts, which gives a measure of the manager, is a basis of our faith in him, and a measure of the financial credit that may be extended to him as a producer. A little consideration will show that such a record is a far safer basis for financial credit in many cases than physical property, and affords a means of financing ability or productive capacity as well as ownership. It is not to be concluded that this subject is being presented in its final and complete form, but it is claimed that enough has been established to enable us to make *an intelligent start in the operation of the new credit system, which the Federal Government was obliged to adopt without any guide.*

Further, it is safe to say that if records such as the ones just described had been available to the prominent business men of the country at the time war broke out, we would have been saved much time, and the expenditure of millions and millions of dollars.

The fact that such a system is applicable to the arts of peace as well as the arts of war; that it will pay for itself while it is being installed; and that it will enable us to value men according to the service they can render, would seem to be sufficient reason why we should lose no more time in taking steps to extend it throughout the nation. This chart system is neither an efficiency nor a scientific management system, as those terms are generally understood. Our system is simply one which enables us to utilize all available information in a manner which is readily understandable to both workmen and executives and has been well received by both. It is designed to enable all of us to use all the knowledge we have to the best advantage, and does not in the slightest interfere with, but rather supplements and supports, the work of those whose problem is to acquire additional knowledge.

In the preceding chapters we have given our view of the economic situation; of the forces that were affecting it, and to what end it was leaning. We have also shown our mechanism for making effective use of all the knowledge available. We also see that with an increase in the amount and availability of knowledge the more certain our course of action is outlined, and the less we need to use opinion or judgment.

In addition, our record charts invariably indicate the most capable men. This not only gives us an indication of how to choose our leaders, but it also provides a continual measure of the effectiveness of their leadership after they are chosen. In this manner we all but eliminate opinion or judgement in the selection of leaders. In doing so, we essentially do away with autocratic methods from whatever source.

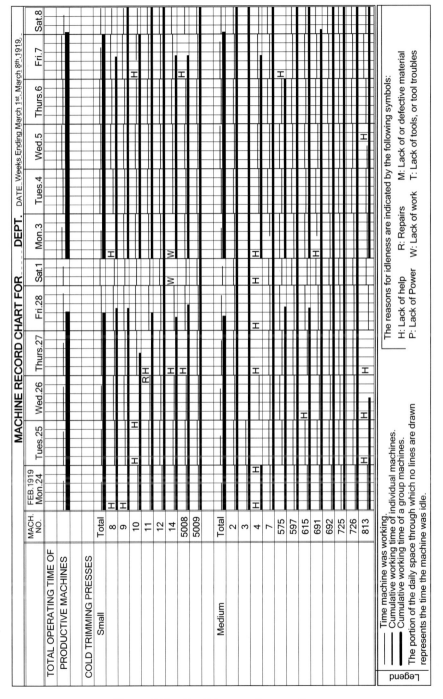

Figure 9 Key For Machine Record Chart

The Religion of Democracy

For over a thousand years the history of the world has been made by two great forces—the church and the state—the church basing its power on idealism and moral forces, the state depending almost entirely upon military power. At times these two forces have seemed for awhile to co-operate, only to become antagonistic towards each other. Today they are absolutely distinct, working in different fields with little common ground while a rival claims center stage. During the last century there has come into the world another force, which has little concern for our religious activities, and interests itself in our political activities only to the extent of making the political forces serve its ends. I speak of the modern business system, based on the tremendously increased productive capacity of the human race due to the advance of the arts and sciences. The rapid expansion of this new power has thrown all our economic mechanism out of gear. The failure of this system in maintaining a social purpose, which is the common thread of the church and state, produces cross-currents and antagonisms in the community which are extremely detrimental to society as a whole.

One hundred years ago, each family — certainly each community — produced nearly everything needed for the simple life then led.

The village blacksmith and the local mill served the community, which existed substantially as a self-contained unit.

With the growth of transportation systems and grand scale production, many of the functions of the local artisans were taken over by the factory, just as the flour mills of Minneapolis supplanted the local mills, which went out of existence.

In the same manner, other large centralized industries by superior service drove out of existence small local industries. By reason of improved machinery and better technology, the centralized industries were able to render this superior service while at the same time securing large profits for themselves. Unfortunately for the country at large, those who came to control these industries did not see that the logical basis of their profits was the service they provided. Only then, when the community as a whole had come to depend solely upon them, did they realized their opportunity for larger profits, and so changed their methods as to give profits first place, oftentimes ignoring almost entirely the subject of service. It is this switch of focus in the business and industrial system, which took place about the close of the nineteenth century, that is the source of much of the woe that has recently come upon the world. Unless the industrial and business system can rapidly recover a sense of service and grant it the first place, it is hard to see what the next few years may bring forth.

The great war through which we have just passed has done away with political autocracy, apparently forever; yet it has done nothing in this country to modify the autocratic methods of our business system. The system is a law unto itself and as such, accepts no definite social responsibility. This force is controlled and operated in the interest of ownership, with little consideration for the interests of those upon whose labor it depends, or for that of the community. We should not be surprised then, that the workman who is most directly affected by this policy is demanding a larger part in the control of industry. The war has taught him, as it has us, that the method of operating an industry is more important to the community than the particular ownership of that industry. The result of this knowledge is that the workers throughout the world are striving everywhere to seize the reins of power. It is unfortunate for the world at large that these workers, as a rule, have no clearer conception of social responsibility than those already in control. More to the point, since these workers have had no experience in operating grand scale industry and business, it is more than likely that their attempt to do so will result disastrously to the community. The industrial system as a whole is thus threatened with a change of control which we can scarcely contemplate with equanimity. We naturally ask if there is any possible relief from the confusion with which we are threatened. We think there is, but not by any of the methods generally advocated by "intellectuals" who are not in touch with the reality of moving forces.

One class believes that the answer comes in governmental ownership and control of industries. However, the experience of the world so far does not give much encouragement along these lines. In some quarters, where public utilities have to a large extent been run by the government, it is frankly admitted that the government is being run by the business system, which leaves us just where we were. *Unless we can get a social purpose into that system*, in which case the need for government ownership would disappear. Is such a thing possible? Unless it can be shown that a business system which has a social purpose is distinctly more beneficial to those who control than one which does not have a social purpose, I frankly confess that there does not seem to be any permanent answer in sight. Be that as it may, if it can be shown conclusively that a business system operated by democratic methods (one which acts without coercion and offers each man the full reward of his labor) is more beneficial to those who lead than the present autocratic system, we have a basis on which to build a modern economic state. We can do this without a revolution, or even a serious jar to our present industrial and business system. In fact, so far as I have been able to put into operation the methods I am advocating, we have very materially reduced the friction and inequalities of the present methods much to the benefit of both employer and employee.

In 1908 I wrote a paper for the American Society of Mechanical Engineers, on "training workmen" in which I used the following expression: "The general policy of the past has been to drive; but the era of force must give way to that of an era of knowledge, and the policy of the future will be to teach and to lead, to the advantage of all concerned."

This sentiment met with much hearty support, but since no mechanism existed for operating industry in such a manner, the sentiment remained for most people just that: a fine sentiment. At that time the organization of which I am the head had already made some advance in the technology of such a system of management, and since that time have continued to develop our methods along the same lines, as shown in the previous chapters of the book.

Throughout this little book we have attempted to make clear that those *who know what to do and how to do it* can most profitably be employed in teaching and training others. In other words, they can earn their greatest reward by rendering service to their fellows as well as to their employers. It is only recently that we have been able to get owners and managers interested in this policy, for all the cost systems of the past have recorded such teachers as non-producers and hence an expense that should not be allowed. Now, however, with a proper cost-keeping system supplemented by a man-record chart system, we see that they are really our most effective producers.

We have attempted in this book to show, by example, the mechanism by which we have put our methods into operation, and some of the results that have been obtained by them. The most important result is that under such a system, no "blind guides" can permanently hold positions of authority, and that leadership automatically gravitates to those who know what to do and how to do it. Moreover, we have yet to find a single place where these methods are not applicable, and where they have not produced better results than the old autocratic system. Furthermore, they produce harmony between employer and employee and are welcomed by both. In other words, *we have proved in many places that the doctrine of service,* which has been preached in the churches as religion, is not only good economics and eminently practical, but because of the increased production of goods obtained by it, promises to lead us safely through the maze of confusion into which we seem to be headed. This doctrine of service is the only thing that can give us that industrial democracy which can afford a basis for industrial peace.

This doctrine has been preached in the churches for nearly two thousand years, and for a while it seemed as if the Catholic Church of the middle ages would make it the controlling factor in the world. Then, the break up of the Church into sects during the middle ages, and the advance of that intellectualism which places more importance upon words and dogma than upon deeds, gave a setback to the idea which has lasted for centuries. Now, when a great catastrophe has made us aware of the futility of such methods, we are beginning to realize that the present business system only needs the simple methods of the Salvation Army to restore it to health. It is absolutely sound at the bottom.

The attempt to run the world by words and phrases for the benefit of those with the power to assemble those words and phrases, involved us in a great war. The continued application of these methods seems to be leading us into deeper and deeper economic confusion. We are therefore compelled to recognize that the methods of the past are no longer possible, and that the methods of the future must be simple and more direct.

It should be perfectly evident that with the increase of complexity of the modern business system (on which modern civilization depends), successful operation can be attained only by following the lead of those who understand practically the controlling forces, and are willing to recognize their social responsibility in operating them.

Any attempt to operate the modern business system by people who do not understand the driving forces is sure to reduce its effectiveness, and any attempt to operate it in the interest of a class is not much longer possible.

For instance, under present conditions the attempt to drive the workman to do that which he does not understand results in failure, even if he is willing to be driven, which he no longer is; for he has learned that real democracy is something more than the privilege of expressing an opinion. As a result of this we are forced into a new economic condition, and whether we like it or not, will soon realize that only those *who know what to do and how to do it* will have a sufficient following to make their efforts worth while. In other words, the conditions under which the great industrial and business system must operate to keep our complicated system of modern civilization going successfully, can be directed only by real leaders — men who understand the operation of the moving forces, and whose prime object is to render such service as the community needs.

In order to secure such leaders they must have full reward for the service they render. This rules out the dollar-a-year man, whose qualifications too often were not that he knew how to do the job, but that he was patriotic and could afford to give his services for nothing. In spite of such a crude way of selecting men to handle problems vital to the life of the nation, many did good work during the war.

The laws of the United States, however, forbid a man to work for the government for nothing, and both those who served at a dollar a year, and those who accepted that service, violated the spirit of the law, according to the service he rendered. Any other practice is undemocratic.

In 1847, Mr. Lincoln wrote: "To secure to each laborer the whole product of his labor or as nearly as possible, is a worthy object of any good government. But then the question arises, how can a government best affect this?" Upon this the habits of our whole species fall into three great classes — useful labor, useless labor, and idleness. Of these, the first only is meritorious, and all the products of labor rightfully belong to it; but the latter two, while they exist, are heavy pensioners upon the first, robbing it of a large portion of its just rights. The only remedy for this is to, so far as possible, drive useless labor and idleness out of existence."

Attempts are always being made to eliminate the idleness of workmen and useless labor by the refusal of compensation. Unfortunately, however, there has been no organized attempt as yet to force capital to be useful by refusing compensation to idle capital, or to capital expended uselessly. Capital which is expended in such a manner as to be non-productive, and capital which is not used, can receive interest only by obtaining the same from capital which was productive or from the efforts of workmen, in either of which cases it gets a reward which it did not earn, and which necessarily comes from capital or labor which did earn it.

Reward according to service rendered is the only foundation on which our industrial and business system can permanently stand. It is a violation of this principle which has created the occasion for socialism, communism, and Bolshevism. All we need to defeat these "isms" is to re-establish our industrial and business system firmly on the principles advocated by Abraham Lincoln in 1847, and we shall establish *an economic democracy that is stronger than any autocracy.*

In addition to what has been said, it conforms absolutely to the teachings of all the churches. It was Christ who was the first to understand the commanding power of service, thereby revealing Him as the first great Economist, for economic democracy is simply applied Christianity. This was also clearly understood by the great leaders of the Church of the Middle Ages, whose failure to establish it as a general practice was largely due to the rise of an intellectualism which disdained practicality.

Now, however, when a great catastrophe has shown us the error of our ways, and convinced us that the world is controlled by deeds rather than words, we see the road to Universal Peace only through the change of Christianity from a weekly intellectual diversion to a daily practical reality.

Index

D

Democracy in Industry 51, 58, 73
Democracy in Management 75
Democracy in Politics xiii
Democracy in the Shop 67
Dollar-a-Year Service 13, 87

E

Economics of Democracy 45
Economic conditions 7, 46
Economic force xi
Economic system xiii, 14, 41, 42, 58
Economists 31, 42, 45
Efficiency and Idleness 25, 35–37, 51
Efficiency Campaign 18–19, 73
Efficiency Methods 73–74
Emergency Fleet Corporation 5, 7, 62
England 47, 52, 53
Europe xiii, 3, 4, 6, 7, 8, 9, 48, 52, 55, 59
Expense of Idleness 19, 35, 37

F

Federal Government 5, 6, 18, 41, 43, 77
Federal Reserve Banking System 40
Financial Credit 67, 68, 77
Financing 5, 13, 41, 43, 77
Food Administration xii
Ford, Henry 41

G

Germany xi, 46, 52, 53, 54
Government Financing 5
Government Ownership 83, 84

O

P

R

S

Soviet System xii, 4, 7, 9, 55, 56
Statisticians 13

T

Theories 6, 23, 24, 32, 33, 46
Training Workmen 69–72, 84
Trusts and Combinatins 2

V

Value of Industrial Property 31–32

W

Wall Street 40
War Labor Board xii

Publications from Enna and PCS Inc.

Enna and PCS Inc. provide companies with publications that help achieve excellence in operations. Enna and PCS Inc. support your efforts to internalize process improvement allowing you to reach your vision and mission. These materials are proven to work in industry. Call toll-free (866) 249-7348 or visit us on the web at www.enna.com to order or request our free product catalog.

Books

Kaizen and the Art of Creative Thinking

Dr. Shingo presents six unique models, the sum of which he calls the Scientific Thinking Mechanism. These frameworks allow groups to deconstruct problems and rebuild them into powerful improvement ideas. This concept is central to Toyota Production System (TPS) and provides the necessary foundation for any Lean Initiative to be built upon.
ISBN 978-1-897363-59-1 | 2007 | $59.40 | Item: **909**

The Strategos Guide to Value Stream & Process Mapping

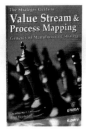

The Strategos Guide to Value Stream and Process Mapping has proven strategies and helpful tips on facilitating group VSM exercises and puts VSM in the greater Lean context. With photos and examples of related Lean practices the book focuses on implementing VSM, not just drawing diagrams and graphs.
ISBN 978-1-897363-43-0 | 2007 | $47.00 | Item: **905**

The Idea Generator, Quickand Easy Kaizen

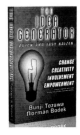

The book discusses the Kaizen mind set that enables a company to utilize its resources to the fullest by directly involving all of its manpower in the enhancement and improvement of the productivity of its operations.
ISBN 978-0971243699 | 2001 | $47.52 | Item: **902**

JIT is Flow

Hirano's *5 Pillars of the Visual Workplace* and *JIT Implementation Manual* were classics. They contained detailed descriptions of techniques and clear instructions. However, Hirano's books were difficult to adapt to many sectors. This book highlights the depth of the thought process behind Hirano's work. The know-how that is contained in this book is extremely useful. The clarity which Hirano brings to JIT/Lean and the delineation of the principles involved will be invaluable to every leader and manager aiming for business excellence.

ISBN 978-0971243613 | 2006 | $47.52 | Item: **903**

Kaikaku, The Power and Magic of Lean

Kai ka ku are Japanese characters meaning a 'transformation of the mind,' Norman Bodek brings his vast cross-cultural experience in Japanese manufacturing systems to American industry and creates proven results. With his first-hand knowledge of Lean Manufacturing origins, Norman Bodek chronicles his introduction to Lean in an easy to read, conversational style text.

ISBN 978-0971243668 | 2006 | $47.52 | Item: **901**

Rebirth of American Industry

We had a certain amount of sadness as we read of the bankruptcy of Delphi Corporation, and the losses and downsizing of General Motors and Ford. The very purpose of this book is to provide modern managers with specific guidelines to be internationally competitive. The book traces the evolution of manufacturing management along two lines: That pioneered by Henry Ford, then furthered by Toyota to its modern level of success; versus that originated by Alfred Sloan and others at General Motors still in practice in most American companies today.

ISBN 978-0971243637 | 2005 | $47.52 | Item: **904**

All You Gotta Do Is Ask

So, after all the committees, review panels, and head scratching, your company has finally started its Lean transformation. *All You Gotta Do Is Ask* explains how to promote a tidal swell of ideas from your employees. This easy-to-read book will show you why it is important to have a good idea system, how to set one up, and what it can do for you, your employees, and your organization.

ISBN 978-0971243651 | 2005 | $47.52 | Item: **906**

Simulations & Training Packages

JIT Factory Flow Kit

This exercise is perfect for companies who have heard of Lean, yet do not fully grasp the power behind it. The JIT Factory Flow Kit is dynamic enough for high-level management training, yet has enough detail for production staff as well. This is our most popular training aid because of the "Ah-ha, I get it!" factor. In less than two hours you will have all your staff agreeing to move to a Lean Production System.

ISBN 978-1-897363-60-7 | 2007 | $47.52 | Item: **1081**

Quick and Easy Kaizen Training Package

Quick and Easy Kaizen is the most effective and powerful way to implement a practical and sustainable employee-led improvement system by encompassing the often-ignored human (employee) side of Lean manufacturing. Enna's Quick and Easy Kaizen is authored by Norman Bodek and made popular by his award winning Shingo Prize book, *Quick and Easy Kaizen: The Idea Generator*.

ISBN 978-1-897363-37-9 | 2006 | $699.99 | Item: **18**

To order: Enna Products Corp. 1602 Carolina St., Unit B3, Bellingham, WA 98229

Overview of Lean Training Package

This package has been designed to create the understanding needed to commit to a Lean Transformation. Make the most of our introductory Lean package by training all your staff in the principles of Lean Manufacturing. Included with this package is a factory flow simulation exercise to demonstrate the concepts of Lean in a real-time exercise. This comprehensive training package is action oriented to ensure successful learning and communication of Lean Manufacturing principles.

ISBN 978-0-973750-92-8 | 2006 | $349.99 | Item: **11**

5S Training Package

Our 5S Solution Packages will help your company create a sustainable 5S program that will turn your shop floor around, and put you ahead of the competition. All of the benefits that come from Lean Manufacturing are built upon a strong foundation of 5S. The success or failure of all improvement initiatives can be traced to the robustness of 5S programs. Enna's solution packages will show you how to implement and sustain an environment of continuous improvement.

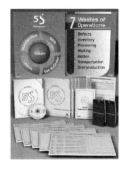

Version 1: ISBN 978-0-973750-90-4 | 2005 | $429.99 | Item: **12**
Version 2: ISBN 978-1-897363-25-6 | 2006 | $429.99 | Item: **17**
Version 1: Sort, Straighten, Sweep, Standardize, and Sustain.
Version 2: Sort, Set In Order, Shine, Standardize, and Sustain

To Order:

Phone, fax, email, or mail to Enna Products Corporation ATTN: Order Processing, 1602 Carolina Street, Unit B3, Bellingham, WA, 98229 USA. Phone: (866) 249-7348, Fax: (905) 481-0756, Email: info@enna.com. Send checks to this address. We accept all major credit cards.

International Orders:

Phone, fax, email, or mail to Enna Products Corporation ATTN: Order Processing, 1602 Carolina Street, Unit B3, Bellingham, WA, 98229 USA. For international calls, Telephone number: +1 (360) 306-5369, Email: info@enna.com, and Facsimile number: +1 (905) 481-0756.

Notice:

All prices are in US dollars and are subject to change without notice.